W9-BKN-286

Pocket
Atlas

Pocket Atlas

PHILIP STEELE

DP

DEMPSEY
PARR

This edition published by Dempsey Parr, 1999
Dempsey Parr is an imprint of Parragon

Parragon, Queen Street House
4 Queen Street
Bath, BA1 1HE, UK

© Copyright Parragon 1998

2 4 6 8 10 9 7 5 3

Produced by Miles Kelly Publishing Ltd,
Bardfield Centre, Great Bardfield, Essex, CM7 4SL

All rights reserved. No part of this publication may be reproduced,
stored in a retrieval system, or transmitted by any means, electronic,
mechanical, photocopying, recording, or otherwise, without the prior
permission of the copyright holder.

British Library Cataloguing-in-Publication Data
A catalogue record for this book is available from the
British Library

Editor: Sean Connolly
Design: Geoff Sida
Cartographic Editor: Keith Lye
Project manager: Kate Miles
Production Assistant: Ian Paulyn
Editorial Assistant: Lynne French

ISBN 1 84084 433 7

Printed in Italy

CONTENTS

HOW TO USE THIS ATLAS

Welcome to the planet Earth! The maps in this atlas show the world we live in. Maps are plans which show the surface of the world as if it were flat, instead of round.

Maps often show the lie of the land and may include mountains, rivers, and seas. Maps that only show these kind of details are called "physical." Maps that only show the borders of countries, states, counties, or provinces

Points of the compass
This symbol represents a compass. The top of the star shows due north, the bottom shows due south.

Land and sea—in color
Colors show the physical details. Green shows lowlands and purple shows mountain Rivers and oceans are marked in blue.

The borders between countries
Red lines show national borders. These South American countries are Colombia, Ecuador, Bolivia, and Peru.

Names and informati
A circle means "town triangle means "mountain". Names a printed in black. The height of a peak is giv in meters above sea le

Where in the world?
If you want to find out where the regional map fits into a map of the whole world, look for the red areas on the globe.

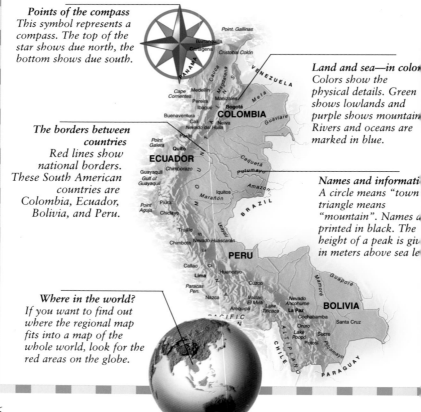

are called "political". The maps in this book show the physical details of the land, but they show national borders and major cities as well.

How do you find the place you are looking for? First of all look up the name you want in the index on p.123. When you have found the right page, look for the name on the map of the region. The little round maps help you to see at a glance which part of the world is being shown. The words will tell you about the countries, the climate of the region and the plants that grow there, the peoples and how they live.

MAKING MAPS

The world is three-dimensional, which means that it can only be shown accurately on a globe. Mapmakers have had to work out clever ways of representing the Earth's curves on flat surfaces such as sheets of paper or computer screens. Some of these methods, called projections, are shown here.

◄ *This projection shows the world in segments as though the map has been peeled off the globe. The shapes always get a bit stretched and distorted when the round world is projected onto a flat surface.*

▲ *Gerardus Mercator in 1538 was the first to depict the world on a flat surface.*

▲ *Peters' projection tries to show the sizes of different countries in proportion to each other.*

WORLD FACT

The Earth is a huge ball of rock and metal, spinning around in space. A line drawn around the middle, or Equator, would measure 24,805 miles. The planet's surface covers an area of about 194,000,000 square miles, of which 71 percent is covered by sea.

Earth Extremes

The lowest exposed part of Earth's surface is in southwest Asia, beside the Dead Sea, at 1,320 feet below sea level.

The world's deepest lake is Baikal, in the Russian Federation. It plunges to 5,367 feet.

About 340 miles of caves and underground passages have been explored in the Mammoth National Park, Kentucky—the world's biggest system.

At 261 miles, the Grand Canyon is the world's longest gorge. It was carved out by the Colorado River in the southwestern United States.

The Ring of Fire is the name given to the borders of the Pacific Ocean, because so many dangerous volcanoes are sited there.

Highest Mountains

Mt. Everest, or Qomolongma, is a spectacular peak in Tibet, on the border between China and Nepal. At 28,995 feet it is higher above sea level than any other mountain.

Mauna Kea, on the Pacific island of Hawaii, measures 33,472 feet from the ocean floor to its peak, which rises to 13,792 feet above sea level.

The highest active volcano in the world rises on the border between Argentina and Chile. It is Ojos del Salado, 22,589 feet high.

The highest range of mountains on any continent is the Himalaya-Karakoram, which includes Mt. Everest and 13 other peaks over 25,000 feet.

AND FIGURES

Longest Rivers

The River Nile flows from Central Africa to the Mediterranean Sea, through the deserts of Egypt. Its natural course is 4,135 miles long.

The River Amazon could be longer than the Nile–it all depends just where you start and finish measuring, for the river has several mouths. It is normally reckoned to be 3,998 miles long. It drains the world's largest surviving area of rain forest.

There is no doubt about which river is in third place. The Chang Jiang (or Yangtze) flows 3,900 miles across central China.

A delta is an area where a river splits into separate waterways before flowing into the ocean. The Ganges-Brahmaputra delta, on the Bay of Bengal, covers about 29,000 square miles.

Oceans

The biggest ocean in the world is the Pacific, with a surface area of 63,939,115 square miles. It is bordered by Asia and Australia to the west and the Americas to the east.

The deepest sea is in the Pacific Ocean. The Marianas Trench, a deep crack in the ocean floor, plunges to a depth of 35,788 feet.

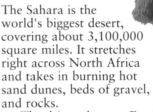

Deserts

The Sahara is the world's biggest desert, covering about 3,100,000 square miles. It stretches right across North Africa and takes in burning hot sand dunes, beds of gravel, and rocks.

The driest place on Earth is probably Chile's Atacama desert, which has almost no rain at any time.

Major Waterfalls

The Angel Falls, or Churun-Meru, have the biggest drop in the world, totaling 3,211 feet. They are in Venezuela, in South America.

The Boyoma Falls, in the Democratic Republic of the Congo, Africa, are the most powerful in the world. They average 600,000 cubic feet of water per second.

Chukchi
Sea

Beaufort
Sea

GREENLAND

Baffin Bay

Arctic Circle

Davis Strait

Denmark Strait

ICELAND

Bering Strait

Hudson Bay

Gulf of
Alaska.

CANADA

IRELAND

Newfoundland

ALEUTIAN ISLANDS

NORTH

PORTUGAL

UNITED STATES OF AMERICA

ATLANTIC

OCEAN

MOROCCO

CANARY
ISLANDS
WESTERN
SAHARA

Gulf of Mexico

Tropic of Cancer

BAHAMAS

HAWAIIAN ISLANDS

MEXICO

CUBA

DOMINICAN
REPUBLIC

MAURITANIA

JAMAICA HAITI

PUERTO RICO

SENEGAL

GUATEMALA BELIZE

Caribbean Sea

GAMBIA
GUINEA-BISSAU

GUINEA

HONDURAS

EL SALVADOR

NICARAGUA

TRINIDAD &
TOBAGO

SIERRA LEONE

LIBERIA

COSTA RICA

PANAMA

VENEZUELA

GUYANA

SURINAME

FRENCH GUIANA

COLOMBIA

Equator

ECUADOR

GALAPAGOS
ISLANDS

SOUTH

ATLANTIC

BRAZIL

OCEAN

PERU

BOLIVIA

PARAGUAY

Tropic of Capricorn

CHILE

URUGUAY

ARGENTINA

FALKLAND/MALVINAS
ISLANDS

South Georgia

Antarctic Circle

SVALBARD

ARCTIC OCEAN

ZEMLYA FRANTSA IOSIFA

SEVERNAYA ZEMLYA

Novaya Zemlya

Barents Sea

Kara Sea

Laptev Sea

NOVOSIBIRSKIYE OSTROVO

East Siberian Sea

SWEDEN FINLAND

ESTONIA

LATVIA

LITHUANIA

RUSSIA

Baltic Sea BELARUS

POLAND

CZECH

REP. SLOVAKIA

USTRIA

HUNGARY

MOLDOVA

ROMANIA

UKRAINE

KAZAKHSTAN

Aral Sea

MONGOLIA

Sea of Okhotsk

Bering Sea

YUGOSLAVIA Black Sea

BULGARIA

ITALY MACEDONIA

ALBANIA

GREECE

GEORGIA

ARMENIA AZERBAIJAN

TURKMENISTAN

KYRGYZSTAN

UZBEKISTAN

TAJIKISTAN

NORTH KOREA

Sea of Japan

PACIFIC

TURKEY

Caspian Sea

CYPRUS SYRIA

LEBANON

ISRAEL

JORDAN

IRAQ

IRAN

AFGHANISTAN

CHINA

SOUTH KOREA JAPAN

Yellow Sea

East China Sea

OCEAN

ranean Sea

SIA

LIBYA

EGYPT

SAUDI

ARABIA

Red Sea

QATAR

UNITED

ARAB

EMIRATES

OMAN

PAKISTAN

NEPAL

BHUTAN

INDIA

BANGLADESH

BURMA

TAIWAN

HONG KONG

Philippine Sea

CHAD

SUDAN

ERITREA YEMEN

Gulf of Aden

ETHIOPIA

Bay of

Bengal

LAOS

THAILAND

VIETNAM

CAMBODIA

South

China

Sea

PHILIPPINES

CENTRAL

AFRICAN

REPUBLIC

OON

NGO ZAIRE UGANDA KENYA

SOMALIA

SRI

LANKA

BRUNEI

MALAYSIA

Celebes

Sea

MELANESIA

RWANDA

BURUNDI

TANZANIA

INDIAN

OCEAN

EAST INDIES

INDONESIA

PAPUA

NEW

GUINEA

SOLOMON

ISLANDS

ANGOLA

ZAMBIA

MALAWI

MOZAMBIQUE

Coral Sea

VANUATU

FIJI

NAMIBIA

ZIMBABWE

BOTSWANA

MADAGASCAR

RÉUNION

MAURITIUS

NEW CALEDONIA

AUSTRALIA

Mozambique Channel

SWAZILAND

LESOTHO

SOUTH AFRICA

Tasman Sea

North I.

NEW

ZEALAND

South I.

ICELAND

Grimsey
Raufarhöfn
Köpasker
Isafjördur
Olafsfjördur
Húsavík
Vopnafjördur
Thingeyri
Hólmavík
Saudárkrókur
Vatneyri
Blönduós
Akureyri
Myvatn
Seyhisfjördur
Neskaupstadur
Olafsvik
Stykkishólmur
Eskifjördur
Budir
Borgarnes
HOFSJÖKULL
Djúpivogur
Akranes
VATNAJÖKULL
Keflavík
Reykjavík
Hekla
Hvannadalshnúkur
Stökkseyri
Heimaey
MYRDALSJÖKULL
Vestmannaeyjar
Vík
Surtsey

ICELAND

FINLAND

SWEDEN

NORWAY

North Cape
Hammerfest
Vadsö
Polmak
Kirkenes
Alta
Utsjoki
Tromsö
Karasjok
Inarijärvi
Mt. Haltia
RUSSIA
L A P L A N D
Narvik
Enontekiö
Kiruna
Mt. Kebnekaise
Vittangi
Sodankylä
Bodö
Gällivare
Pelkosenniemi
Jokkmokk
Rovaniemi
Boden
Tornio
Kemi
Mosjöen
Sorsele
Luleå
Storuman
Skellefte
Piteå
Oulu
Skellefteå
Kajaani
Namsos
Grong
Dorotea
Ume
Bygdeå
Kokkola
Outokumpu
NORWEGIAN
Steinkjer
Umeå
Jakobstad
FINLAND
SEA
Trondheim
Örnsköldsvik
Kuopio
Joensuu
Kristiansund
Östersund
Vaasa
Ålesund
Sunndalsöra
Kramfors
Seinäjoki
Jyväskylä
Röros
Dombås
Sundsvall
Tampere
Galdhöpiggen
Ljusdal
Pori
Säma
Hudiksvall
Rauma
Hämeenlinna
Kouvola
NORWAY
Lillehammer
Bollnäs
Söderhamn
Lahti
Voss
Mora
Hyvinkää
Kotka
Bergen
Gjövik
Falun
Gävle
Helsinki
Borlänge
ÅLAND
Turku
Uskedal
Västerdal
Uppsala
Mariehamn
Haugesund
Drammen
Västerås
Oslo
Stavanger
Skien
Fredrikstad
Karlstad
Örebro
Stockholm
Larvik
Eskilstuna
Södertälje
Egersund
Strömstad
Arendal
Vänern
Norrköping
Mandal
Kristiansand
Uddevalla
Linköping
Trollhättan
Vättern
GOTLAND
Skagerrak
Göteborg
Borås
Jönköping
Västervik
Visby
Ålborg
Växjö
Borgholm
Holstebro
Viborg
Kattegat
Halmstad
Kalmar
ÖLAND
JUTLAND
Randers
Horsens
Århus
Helsingborg
Karlskrona
Esbjerg
Kristianstad
DENMARK
Malmö
Kolding
Copenhagen
Ystad
Bornholm
Odense
Trelleborg
Rönne
GERMANY

ICELAND

FINLAND

SWEDEN

NORWAY

SWEDEN

DENMARK

STOP FOR

DENMARK

THE FAR NORTH

The lands of Europe's far north include the Scandinavian countries of Denmark, Sweden, and Norway. Finland lies to the east and Iceland far to the west, in the North Atlantic Ocean. All these countries except Denmark border the Arctic Circle, but their waters are warmed by ocean currents.

Two large peninsulas stick out from the mainland of northwestern Europe, like the pincers of a giant crab. They divide the North Sea from the Baltic. The southern peninsula is the smaller one, which extends northward from Germany. It is called Jutland. Together with the nearby islands of Fyn, Lolland, Falster, and Sjælland it makes up the kingdom of Denmark. Most of Denmark is flat and low-lying, a country of green farmland. The Danish capital, Copenhagen, is on Sjælland and is home to more than 1.3 million people. A further 4 million Danes live in the rest of this small country. Denmark exports bacon and dairy products. This is the most southerly Scandinavian country, with the mildest climate.

Denmark also rules the Faeroe Islands and distant Greenland, although these territories now have their own parliaments

and make their own laws.

Across the windy channels of Skagerrak and Kattegat, between the North Sea and the Baltic, is the long Scandinavian peninsula, which stretches northwards, beyond the Arctic Circle. The landscape of this part of Europe was shaped by movements of ice in prehistoric times. Glaciers carved out the deep sea inlets called fiords along the ragged western coast. Ranges of mountains run down the Scandinavian peninsula like a backbone. They descend to a land of spruce and birch forests, bogs and thousands of sparkling lakes. Scandinavia is the home of reindeer, elk, brown bear, and salmon.

Summers can be warm, but winters are bitterly cold, with heavy snow. Cross-country skiing and other winter sports are popular. In Arctic regions the midsummer sun shines through much of the night, while the days of midwinter are dark, lit up only by the eerie

◀ **Taking a trolley ride**
A trolley squeals through the streets of Helsinki, the Finnish capital. Trolleys are still a popular means of transportation in many northern European cities.

flickering of the northern lights, known as aurora borealis, in the sky.

Norway occupies the western half of the Scandinavian peninsula. This is a harsh landscape with few resources apart from timber and water, so the Norwegians have always had to turn seaward to survive. They live by fishing, and North Sea production platforms also make Norway the largest producer of oil and natural gas in western Europe. The Norwegian capital, Oslo, lies in the south of the country. The population of the country as a whole is 4.4 million. Norway's North Cape, or Nordkapp, is the northernmost point in the whole of Europe. Norway also rules two Arctic territories— Jan Mayen island and the Svalbard archipelago.

Sweden occupies the eastern and southern part of the Scandinavian peninsula, with its capital at Stockholm. This city is an old trading port built over islands linked by bridges. Sweden has the highest population of these northern lands, at 8.9 million. It is a major exporter of timber, paper, wooden furniture, and motor vehicles. It uses its rivers to power hydroelectric schemes and has reserves of iron ore, copper, silver, and uranium. The southern part of the country has fertile farmland which produces grain and root crops.

Iceland is an independent country with strong

◄ Copenhagen's Little Mermaid
This statue at the water's edge shows a character made famous over a century ago by Danish fairy tale writer Hans Christian Andersen.

historical links to mainland Scandinavia. It is a sparsely populated island of bleak moors, mountains, glaciers and snow fields, volcanoes, warm springs, and geysers— spouts of water which gush up from underground. Many Icelanders live by fishing and by farming. The same energy which heats the island's hot springs provides power to heat homes and greenhouses, where vegetables and flowers can be grown.

Today's Danes, Swedes, Norwegians, and Icelanders are all closely related, and so are the

◄ Fiords of the Vikings
Snow-capped mountains and sheer rocks plunge into the still, deep waters of Nordfiord, near the Norwegian village of Hopland.

▲ *Hand weaving in Småland*
A weaver works at her loom in the Småland region of southern Sweden. All the Scandinavian countries have a long tradition of arts and crafts.

various Germanic languages that they speak. It was from Scandinavia that the seafarers known as Vikings set out about 1,200 years ago. The Vikings raided and settled the coasts of Western Europe, traded in Russia and the Middle East, settled Iceland and Greenland, and even reached North America.

Not all northern Europeans are descended from the Vikings. The Arctic lands of northern Scandinavia are known as Lapland and are home to the Saami, a people who traditionally led nomadic lives, following their herds of reindeer to their pastures. Some are still herders, while others have found more settled work.

The 5 million Finns are not

ST. LUCIA'S DAY

In the dark days of the Scandinavian winter, many festivals are held which celebrate light and warmth. St. Lucia, or Lucy, is the Christian saint of light. Her feast day is December 13 and it is celebrated in Sweden by girls wearing candles and wreathes of green leaves on their heads.

related to any of the other peoples in the region. Finland borders the Russian Federation and has coasts on the Gulf of Bothnia and the Gulf of Finland, which are long arms of the Baltic Sea. It has thousands of lakes and its evergreen forests make it a leading producer of wood pulp and paper. Helsinki is the northernmost capital on the European mainland. Finland was ruled by Sweden in the Middle

▲ *Marching through Copenhagen*
Young members of the Tivoli Guard Marching Band parade through the Tivoli Gardens. They wear red and white, the Danish national colors.

Ages, and by Russia from 1809 until 1917.

Most of the peoples of Europe's far north are Lutheran Christians. Denmark, Norway, and Sweden are all monarchies, ruled by kings or queens. Finland and Iceland are both republics. Denmark, Sweden, and Finland are trading partners within the European Union (EU), but Norway voted against joining this economic and political alliance in 1994.

West Frisian Islands

Ameland

Terscheling

Vlieland

Leeuwarden

Groningen

Waddenzee

Texel

Barrier Dam

Sneek

Assen

Em

IJsselmeer

North-East
Polder

Meppel

Alkmaar

Markerwaard
Polder
(planned)

Flevoland
Polder

Zwolle

Zaanstad

Almelo

Haarlem

Amsterdam

NETHERLANDS

NETHERLANDS

Hilversum

En

Leiden

Amersfoort

Apeldoorn

IJssel

The Hague

Gouda

Utrecht

Delft

Lek

Arnhem

Rotterdam

Waal

Nijmegen

Dordrecht

Maas

GERMANY

s'Hertogenbosch

Oosterschelde

Breda

Tilburg

Vlissingen

Eindhoven

Westerschelde

Venlo

Zeebrugge

Ostend

Bruges

Antwerp

St. Niklaas

Genk

Heerlen

Ghent

Mechelen

Hasselt

Maastricht

Roeslare

Kortijk

Aalst

Brussels

Leuven
(Louvain)

Liège

Vaalserberg

Schelde

Waterloo

Verviers

BELGIUM

Huy

Meuse

Spa

Botrange

Tournai

La Louvière

Sambre

Namur

FRANCE

Mons

Charleroi

ARDENNES
MOUNTAINS

Dinant

Buurgplatz

GERMANY

Bastogne

Libramont

LUXEMBOURG

Luxembourg

Esch-sur-Alzette

NETHERLANDS

BELGIUM

LOW COUNTRIES

Between Germany and France, the North Sea coast is made up of sand dunes, islands, and estuaries. The land is very low and at the mercy of storms and severe flooding. The flat fields of the Netherlands and Belgium rise in the south to the Ardennes hills and the little country of Luxembourg.

The country of the Netherlands is sometimes called Holland, but that is really the name of just two of its provinces, North and South Holland. "Nether" means "low" and this is the lowest, flattest part of northern Europe. Long barriers and sea defences have been built to protect the countryside from North Sea floods. Large areas of land called polders have been reclaimed from the sea over the ages. The Dutch landscape is

green, crisscrossed by canals and dikes, tree-lined roads and bridges, and modern highways. Many old windmills, which were built to pump the polders dry, may still be seen.

After a period under Spanish rule, the Netherlands became wealthy in the 1600s by trading with Southeast Asia. Its capital city, Amsterdam, still has many beautiful old houses and canals dating back to this golden age. Amsterdam is a lively city which attracts young people from all over Europe. It is ringed by modern suburbs. There are many other fine old towns and cities. The Dutch have a long tradition of art and design. The work of painters such as Rembrandt van Rijn (1606-1669) and

◀ Beside the North Sea
The seafaring tradition of the Netherlands dates back to the 1600s. This is the old harbor at Hoorn in North Holland.

Vincent van Gogh (1853-1890) may be seen in museums and galleries.

The Netherlands today remain a center of commerce, exporting beers, tulips and other bulbs, cut flowers, tomatoes and vegetables as well

▲ Old times remembered
Traditional costume may still be seen at festivals in some coastal regions and islands of the Netherlands.

as dairy products, especially cheese. Industry is concentrated in the south, producing electrical and household goods. The city of Rotterdam is the world's busiest seaport.

Dutch people make up the biggest part of the population, which numbers about 15.6 million. In the far north and on offshore islands are the closely related Frisian people, who have their own language. The country is also home to many people whose families came from former Dutch colonies in Indonesia and Surinam, as well as immigrants from Turkey and southern Europe. The majority of people are Christians, belonging to both the Roman Catholic and Protestant traditions.

The Flemish people of Belgium are closely related to the Dutch and their two languages are very similar. Belgium is also home to a French-speaking people, the Walloons, who mostly live in the south of the country. Language and cultural differences have given rise to conflict between the two communities over the years. Both Flemish and French are official languages. The total population of Belgium is about 10.2 million. Most Belgians are Roman Catholics.

The north of the country is densely populated, with the capital centrally located at Brussels. Much of the Belgian countryside is also very low and flat, with large areas of polder. It is crossed by the rivers Schelde (also known as Escaut or Scheldt), Meuse (or Maas) and Sambre. The land rises to the south, where the wooded hills of the Ardennes rise above old stone-built towns and villages.

Belgium is heavily industrialized, producing steel, chemicals, plastics, paints, and fertilizers. It was formerly an important coal-mining region. The country is also known for its fine foods. Chocolates, pâtés, spicy sausages, hams, and

traditional strong beers are all exported. Ghent and Bruges have produced textiles since the Middle Ages.

Luxembourg is a tiny country, a survivor of the age when most of Europe was divided into little states, principalities, and duchies. However, modern industry and banking have made Luxembourg the wealthiest country in Europe. The Ardennes cross its northern region, while the south is rich farmland. In the east, on the German border, are the steeply banked vineyards of the Moselle valley. The people of Luxembourg speak French, German, and a local language called Letzebuergesch.

Belgium and the Netherlands are both monarchies and Luxembourg is ruled by a Grand Duke. The three countries have close ties. In 1948, after the terrible years of the Second World War (1939-1945), Belgium, the Netherlands and Luxembourg set up an economic union called "Benelux." It prospered and in 1957 they went on to become

▼ Theme park
Hurtling through the water, these children enjoy getting soaked on the Rada river at Alibi fun park, Belgium.

three of the six countries which founded what is now the European Union (EU). Many EU organizations are now based in the region. Brussels, the Belgian capital, is headquarters of the EU Council and Commission, and Luxembourg City is the home of the European Court of Justice and the secretariat of the European Parliament.

▼ Sails in the wind
The sails of windmills rise from the flat, green farmland of South Holland, at Stompwijk near Gouda.

THE FEAR OF FLOODS

Nearly 2,000 people died along the coast of the Netherlands in 1953, when the North Sea storms caused dreadful flooding. The engineers' answer to tragedies such as this was the Delta Project, which was completed in 1986. It was decided to dam three river mouths and to build a huge barrier, more than 5 miles long, across the East Scheldt river. Today, whenever the sea levels rise, 62 steel gates are raised against the floods.

▶ Wren
This tiny bird, with its distinctive cocked tail, can be seen all over Great Britain.

SHETLAND ISLANDS
Yell
Unst
Foula
Lerwick
Sumburgh Head
Fair Isle

NORTH SEA

Westray
ORKNEY ISLANDS
Kirkwall
Hoy
South Ronaldsay
Cape Wrath
John o'Groats
Thurso

SCOTLAND

Butt of Lewis
Stornoway
Lewis
NORTH WEST HIGHLANDS
OUTER HEBRIDES
North Uist
Moray Firth
Fraserburgh
Peterhead
Skye
Inverness
Loch Ness
Spey
Don
Aberdeen
South Uist
Dee
INNER HEBRIDES
Rhum
Mallaig
Ben Nevis ▲
GRAMPIAN MTS.
Montrose
Barra
Coll
Tiree
Mull
Oban
Perth
SIDLAW HILLS
Dundee
Loch Lomond
Forth
OCHIL HILLS
Firth of Forth
Jura
Greenock
Glasgow
Edinburgh
St. Abbs Head
Islay
Kilmarnock
Clyde
SCOTLAND
Berwick-upon-Tweed
Holy I.
Kintyre Pen.
Arran
Ayr
Tweed
Jedburgh
CHEVIOT HILLS
Tory I.
Malin Head
Rathlin I.
NORTH
SOUTHERN UPLANDS
Newcastle upon Tyne
Aran I.
Londonderry
Giants Causeway
ANTRIM
CHANNEL
Dumfries
Carlisle
Solway Firth
Durham
Sunderland
ENGLAND

ATLANTIC OCEAN

NORTHERN IRELAND

DONEGAL MTS.
SPERRIN MTS.
Lough Neagh
Stranraer
Lake District
PENNINES
Tyne
Middlesbrough
Erris Head
Donegal Bay
Donegal
Lower Lough Erne
Belfast
Scafell Pike
NORTH YORK MOORS
Scarborough
Flamborough Head
Achill Head
Lough Conn
Sligo
Upper Lough Erne
Armagh
Slieve Donard ▲
Isle of Man
Swale
Leeds
York
Clew Bay
Lough Mask
Lough Allen
Dundalk
Douglas
Walney I.
Morecambe Bay
Preston
Bradford
Kingston upon Hull
Lough Corrib
Lough Ree
Boyne
IRISH SEA
Blackpool
Ouse
Wigan
Oldham
Spurn Head
Galway Bay
Athlone
Liffey
Dublin
Anglesey
Liverpool
Manchester
Sheffield
Rotherham
LINCOLN WOLDS
ARAN ISLANDS
IRELAND
Shannon
BOG OF ALLEN
Lough Derg
Dun Laoghaire
Holyhead
Llandudno
Wrexham
Derby
Nottingham
Trent
The Wash
Loop Head
Carlow
WICKLOW MTS.
Wicklow Head
Caernarfon Bay
Snowdon ▲
CAMBRIAN MTS.
Stoke on Trent
Leicester
THE FENS
Norwich
Limerick
Tipperary
Nore
Barrow
Wexford
Bardsey I.
Wolverhampton
Walsall
Peterborough
EAST ANGLIA
Gt. Blasket I.
GALTY MTS.
Waterford
Cardigan Bay
Birmingham
Severn
Coventry
Northampton
Cambridge
Ipswich
Dingle Bay
Carrauntoohill ▲ 1,041 m
Blackwater
Killarney
Hook Head
Aberystwyth
WALES
Wye
Milton Keynes
Kenmare River
Bantry
Cork
Cardigan
Carmarthen
Cheltenham
COTSWOLD HILLS
Oxford
CHILTERNS
Luton
Colchester
Bantry Bay
Mizen Head
Old Head of Kinsale
St. Brides Bay
Swansea
Newport
Gloucester
Swindon
Reading
Thames
London
Southend-on-Sea
Chelmsford
REPUBLIC OF IRELAND
Milford Haven
Gower Peninsula
Cardiff
Bristol
Basingstoke
NORTH DOWNS
Canterbury
Bristol Channel
MENDIP HILLS
Salisbury
HAMPSHIRE DOWNS
Winchester
THE WEALD
Folkestone
Lundy
Ilfracombe
EXMOOR
Bridgwater
Southampton
SOUTH DOWNS
Hastings
WALES
Bude
DARTMOOR
Exeter
Bournemouth
Portsmouth
Brighton
Torbay
Portland Bill
Isle of Wight
ENGLISH CHANNEL
Plymouth
St. Ives
Penzance
ISLES OF SCILLY
Lands End
Lizard Point

Alderney
CHANNEL ISLANDS
Guernsey
Jersey

BRITISH ISLES

The British Isles lie off the northwestern coast of Europe, between the shallow waters of the North Sea and the stormy Atlantic Ocean. Their western shores are warmed by an ocean current called the North Atlantic Drift. The climate is mild, with a high rainfall in the west.

The largest of the British Isles is called Great Britain, and its three countries (England, Scotland, and Wales) are joined within the United Kingdom (UK). The second largest of the British Isles is Ireland. Most of Ireland is an independent republic, but part of the north is governed as a province of the United Kingdom.

Several islands off the shore of Great Britain are self-governing, but have the British monarch as head of state and close political links with the UK. These include the Channel Islands, off the coast of France, and the Isle of Man in the Irish Sea.

About 80 percent of the UK population lives in England, the largest of the three countries within the United Kingdom. It takes up the southern part of

▲ *Travelers' caravan, Ireland.*
A perfect way to see the green landscape of the Emerald Isle.

Great Britain. The southeast is densely populated and includes the city of London, on the River Thames. London is the capital and has a population of more than 8 million. The chief shopping districts and the Houses of Parliament lie in the west, while the City district to the east is a center of finance.

England's south coast takes in the grasslands of the Salisbury Plains and the major ports of Southampton, Portsmouth, and Plymouth. In the southwest, the long rocky peninsula of Cornwall extends toward

▼ *Historical towns and villages*
Half-timbered houses may still be seen at Stratford-upon-Avon, the home town of the great English playwright William Shakespeare (1564-1616).

the Scilly Islands in the Atlantic Ocean. The flat lowlands of East Anglia produce wheat and vegetables, while the Midlands are mostly industrial. Birmingham is the second largest city in the UK. Northern England is dominated by the hill country of the Pennines and the Yorkshire moors and by the lakes of Cumbria. Major northern ports include Liverpool in the west and Newcastle upon Tyne in the east.

Wales is a land of mountains and uplands, which descend through green valleys to coastal lowlands. It raises sheep and cattle. The large Welsh coal mining and slate quarrying industries have declined, but have been replaced to some extent by factories producing electronics and consumer goods. The capital is Cardiff, in the industrial southeast.

Scotland has the highest mountain ranges of the British Isles, fertile lowlands, and long lakes, or lochs. Offshore are many island chains, including the Hebrides and the Orkneys. The capital is Edinburgh, in the east. It is dominated by a high castle, and is famous for its international arts festival. Glasgow is Scotland's largest city, an industrial centre on the River Clyde.

Ireland is a less crowded island than Great Britain. It has rolling green fields, expanses of peat bog, misty hills, lakes, and rivers. In the west, steep cliffs are pounded by Atlantic breakers. The capital of the Irish Republic, Dublin, lies in the east of the country, on the River Liffey. It is an attractive city with many fine houses from the 1700s and 1800s. The Northern Irish capital is the industrial city of Belfast.

▲ *Harvest time in the wheat fields*
The landscapes of the British Isles have been shaped by thousands of years of farming. Food products are major exports from both Great Britain and Ireland.

▶ *Conwy castle, North Wales*
The Welsh fought against English and Norman invaders for over 800 years. This massive castle was built by their fiercest enemy, the English King Edward I, in the 1280s.

◄ Loch Awe, in western Scotland
This is the longest freshwater loch in Scotland, lying beneath the mountain of Ben Cruachan and the ruins of Kilchurn Castle.

▼ The heart of London
Piccadilly Circus lies at the heart of London's West End. Its famous statue is meant to be an angel, but is better known as Eros (the Greek god of love).

It was in the British Isles that the Industrial Revolution —the age of factories and machines—first started in the 1700s and 1800s. Today both the United Kingdom and Ireland are members of the European Union (EU). Farming is important throughout the British Isles, but service industries such as banking, insurance, and tourism have largely overtaken manufacturing. Resources include rich oilfields in the North Sea.

English is spoken throughout the British Isles, but other languages may be heard too – Welsh, Irish and Scots Gaelic, and the various languages spoken by British people of Asian and African descent. The Welsh, Cornish, Scots, and Irish are mostly of Celtic descent, while many of the English are descended from Anglo-Saxons, a Germanic people who invaded England about 1,500 years ago.

In the Middle Ages, England came to dominate its neighbors in the British Isles. Together they went on to rule the largest overseas empire the world has ever seen. In the 1900s the British Empire rapidly declined. Nearer home, Ireland started on the road to independence in 1921, although continuing British rule in the north caused a violent conflict which survives today. Both Scotland and Wales voted in separate referendums for greater control over their own affairs in 1997.

The British Isles have produced some of the world's greatest literature and have also been very influential in popular music. Popular sports first played in Britain include association football (soccer), rugby union, rugby league, cricket, and tennis.

► **What's on the menu?**
*Dishes of the day are chalked up on
the window of a Parisian restaurant.
Many people believe French food to be
the best in the world.*

MONACO

FRANCE

Dunkerque
Calais
Boulogne   Lille   **BELGIUM**
Montreuil Arras   Douai   **LUXEMBOU**
Abbeville   Valenciennes
Dieppe   St. Quentin   Cambrai   Hirson
Amiens   Charleville-Mézières
Cherbourg   Bay of   Fécamp   Montdidier
the Seine   Bolbec   Compiègne   Reims   **Meuse**   Verdi
Le Havre   Rouen   Beauvais
Carentan   Caen   Louviers   *Seine*   Châlons-sur-Marne   **Marne**
St. Lô   Lisieux   Evreux   **Paris**   Meaux
Gulf of St-Malo   Granville   Argentan   Versailles
Morlaix   St.-Malo   St. Germain-en-Laye   Rambouillet   St.Dizier
Brest   St-Brieuc   Dinan   Fontainebleau   **NORMANDY HILLS**
Fougeres   Alençon   Chartres   Nemours   *Seine*
Douarnenez   Mayenne   Troyes
Quimper   Pontivy   Rennes   Vitre   Laval   Orléans   Sens
Lorient   Le Mans   Montargis   Auxerre   Langres
Vannes   *Loire*   Gien   **LANGRES PLAT**
Redon   Angers   Blois
St. Nazaire   Tours   Avallon   Dijon
Belle-Ile   Nantes   Saumur   Vierzon   *Loire*   **Di**
Châtellerault   *Cher*   Bourges   Nevers   Autun
La Roche-sur-Yon   Châteauroux   Le Creuso   Chalon-su
Isle d'Yeu   Poiters   La Châtre   Montceau les Mines   St.C
Les Sables-d'Olonne   Niort   Moulins   Mâcon   *Saône*
Ré I.   Montluçon   Bourg-en-Bresse
La Rochelle   Civray   **F R A N C E**   Vichy   Villefranches
Rochefort   Lyon   Villeurba
Oléron I.   Limoges   Clermont-Ferrand   ▲ Puy de Sancy   Cham
Royan   Cognac   Angoulême   Vienne
Pauillac   Nontron   **MASSIF**   St.-Etienne   Annonay
Barbezieux   **CENTRAL**   Romans-sur-Ise
Périgueux   Aurillac   Prives   Valence
Libourne   Souillac   *Cère*   Montélimar
Bordeaux   Bergerac   *Dordogne*   **CEVENNES**   **RHONE**
Marmande   *Lot*   Rodez   Mende   *Lot*
LES   Cahors   *Aveyron*   Millau   Avignon   Carp
LANDES   Agen   Montauban   Albi   *Tarn*   Nîmes   *Durar*
Monte-de-Marsan   Gaillac   **LANGUE**   Arles
Bayonne   *Adour*   Auch   Toulouse   Montpellier
Biarritz   Castres   Carcassonne   Béziers   Sète   Mars
Pau   *Garonne*   *Ariège*   Narbonne
Tarbes   **PYRENEES**   *Aude*   Foix   Perpignan
Lourdes   St. Gaudens
SPAIN   **ANDORRA**

Cape Corse

Bastia

Gulf of Sagone   **CORSICA**

Ajaccio

Bonifacio
Strait of Bonifacio

FRANCE
AND MONACO

France is one of the larger countries of western Europe. It forms a bridge between the north and south of the continent, with coasts on the cool English Channel, the stormy Atlantic Ocean and the warm, blue Mediterranean Sea. Monaco is a tiny independent principality on its southern coast.

France is a beautiful country lying at the heart of western Europe. Its limate is cool and temperate in the north, and warm and dry in the south. The population numbers about 58.6 million.

Western regions include the massive peaks of the Pyrenees, vineyards and pine forests, peaceful rivers, and sandy shores along the Bay of Biscay. The north includes the stormy headlands of Brittany, the cliffs of Normandy, and the Channel ports. Rolling fertile plains are drained by the winding River Seine, over whose banks and islands sprawls the French capital. Paris is one of the world's great cities, with broad avenues, historic palaces and churches, and the famous landmark of the Eiffel Tower, a high iron pinnacle erected in 1889. The east of France is bordered by the wooded hills of the Ardennes and the Vosges, which stretch southward to the high forested slopes of the Jura mountains and finally the spectacular glaciers and ridges of the Alps. Mont Blanc is the highest peak in western Europe, at 15,767 feet above sea level.

The rocks of the Massif Central, shaped by ancient volcanoes, rise in central southern France, to the west of the Rhône valley. Here too are many famous vineyards. The sun-baked hills of southern France border the warm waters of the Mediterranean Sea. This coast includes the wetlands of the Camargue, famous for their wild horses and varied bird life, as well as the great seaport of Marseilles and the fashionable yachting marinas of Cannes. The sunny south coast and uplands make up a region known as Provence, which attracts many tourists. The Mediterranean island of Corsica, which lies to the southeast, is also

ruled by France.

France has long played a major part in world history, from the Middle Ages onward. During the reign of Louis XIV (1638-1715) it became the most powerful and influential country in Europe. The French Revolution of 1789 saw the violent overthrow of the king and the ruling classes. A general called Napoleon Bonaparte had himself crowned emperor in 1804 and conquered large areas of Europe, before being defeated by British and Prussian troops in 1815.

The French language is still spoken in those parts of the world that formerly made up France's large overseas empire, built up in the 1700s and 1800s. These include large areas of Africa, the Caribbean, and the Québec province of Canada. French is spoken throughout France, although there are many strong dialects and several separate minority languages.

The French people are descended from a Celtic people called the Gauls and also

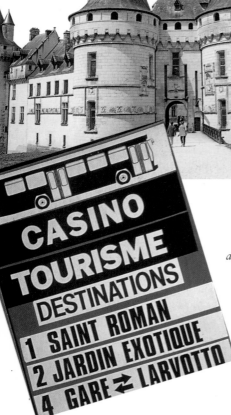

▲ *Château de Chaumont*
This is one of many fairytale castles and stately homes built in the valley of the River Loire. This picturesque region attracts many visitors to its fine scenery and beautiful cuisine.

◄ *Next stop, the Casino...*
Take a bus to the casino in Monte Carlo, and you may come back in a Rolls Royce! Fortunes are won and lost in the capital of Monaco.

◀ **Market produce**
Fresh produce is the key to good cooking. The French countryside produces apples, pears, and cherries, and choice vegetables such as beans, peas, asparagus, and artichokes.

from Germanic peoples such as the Franks and the Vikings (who settled in Normandy). Within France are several other peoples with their own languages and

THE WORLD'S FINEST WINES
Grape vines are trimmed at Saint Hippolyte, in Alsace. France has been producing wines since Roman times and its regions have given their name to many world-famous wines, such as Burgundy, Bordeaux, and Champagne. Cognac makes the finest brandy — a strong liquor also made from grapes.

distinct cultures, such as the Bretons (another branch of Celts, who are closely related to the Cornish and Welsh of Great Britain), the Basques and the Catalans (whose homeland stretches into Spain), the Alsatians, and the Corsicans. Algerians and other North African peoples have also settled in France. About 90 percent of z with most of the remainder being Protestant Christians, Muslims, or Jews.

Modern France, which suffered invasions by Germany during the World Wars of 1914-1918 and 1939-1945, is a republic. It has been working for European unity since the 1950s and is a key member of the European Union (EU). As a major industrial power it produces cars, aerospace equipment, chemicals, and textiles. The country is also renowned for its wines, its cheeses, its fine cooking or haute cuisine, and the great fashion houses of Paris. France has produced many of the world's greatest writers, painters, musicians, scientists, and film-makers.

A section of the Mediterranean coast is occupied by a very small principality called Monaco. This has close links with its large neighbor and shares the same currency, the franc. Most of this state is taken up by the city of Monte Carlo, famous for its casino and the annual Monaco Grand Prix Formula 1 motor racing event.

GERMANY

AUSTRIA

SWITZERLAND

LIECHTENSTEIN

GERMANY
AND THE ALPS

Germany extends southward from the windy coasts of the North Sea and the Baltic to the snowy peaks of the Alps, in the southern region of Bavaria (Bayern). The Alps form the biggest mountain chain of Western Europe and are taken up by three other countries—Switzerland, Austria, and tiny Liechtenstein.

Germany lies between Western and Central Europe. Its western regions, or Länder, take in the Black Forest and the Rivers Rhine and Moselle, which wind through steep valleys planted with vines. Its eastern Länder flank the Bohemian Forest, the Ore Mountains (Erzgerbirge) and the Rivers Oder and Neisse.

▲ *Dream castle for a mad king*
Romantic Neuschwanstein Castle was built in the 1870s for the mad King Ludwig II of Bavaria.

Germany's northern coasts are made up of sand dunes and offshore islands. The Baltic and North Sea sections are linked by the busy waterway of the Kiel Canal. Northern Germany is flat, mainly crossed by great rivers such as the Elbe and Weser. Major ports include Bremen, Hamburg, Lübeck, and Rostock.

The northwest includes the industrial belt around the Ruhr river, which flows into the Rhine at Duisburg. The northeast takes up part of a great plain which stretches eastward into Poland and Russia. On its edge, set among forests and lakes, is the capital city of Berlin.

In central Germany, the landscape rises from sandy heaths and moors to the highlands of the Harz mountains. Two great rivers, the Main and the Danube, cross the southern half of the country, which rises toward the high peaks of the Bavarian Alps. Germany has many large, modern industrial or commercial cities, such as Frankfurt-am-Main and Stuttgart, as well as pretty villages,

▲ Fine wines
Perfect soil and weather conditions in the Rhine valley make wine production a huge industry in Germany.

cathedrals, and ruined castles dating back to the Middle Ages.

For most of its history Germany has been divided into different states. In the Middle Ages the country was a patchwork of small nations and cities. Many of them were part of a federation called the Holy Roman Empire. In the 1700s the northeastern kingdom of Prussia became the most powerful of the German states.

Germany united as a single empire in 1870, but it was

disastrously defeated in World War I (1914-1918). A dictator called Adolf Hitler, leader of the racist Nazi Party, came to power in the 1930s. During World War II (1939-1945) he ordered the invasion of most of Europe as well as the murder of millions of Jews, Gypsies, and political opponents in death camps.

Defeated again, Germany and the city of Berlin were divided into two, between the communist east and the capitalist west.

It was 1990 before Germany was reunited. Germany today is a federal republic, with considerable powers devolved to the Länder. It is a leading member of the European Union and is a major world producer of cars, electrical and household goods, medicines, and chemicals.

Despite its troubled history, Germany has been home to many of Europe's greatest thinkers, writers, artists, and musical composers – Johann Wolfgang von Goethe was born in Frankfurt-am-Main in 1749 and

TASTY FARE

Germany is famous for its wines and its beers, and is said to produce more than 1,500 different kinds of sausage. Bread is made from rye as well as wheat and popular dishes include veal and pork. The most famous Swiss dish is fondue, Gruyère or Emmentaler cheese melted in a pot with white wine, kirsch, pepper and garlic. Forks of bread are dipped into the sauce. Vienna, the Austrian capital is famous for delicious tarts and cakes served with coffee and cream.

▲ **Swiss chalets, snowy peaks**
Traditional "chalets," timber houses with broad roofs, may be seen in the villages around Lake Thun, in Switzerland.

Ludwig van Beethoven in Bonn in 1770.

Switzerland is a small, wealthy country set among the lakes and snowy peaks of the Alps and the Jura ranges. Its beautiful landscape and historical towns attract many tourists. In all the Alpine countries there are pretty villages of wooden houses built with wide, sloping roofs designed to withstand the heavy winter snowfall. Swiss industries include dairy produce, precision instruments, and finance. Zurich is a world center of banking, while Geneva is the headquarters of many international agencies, such as the Red Cross and the World Health Organization.

To the east, the tiny country of Liechtenstein is closely linked with Switzerland and uses the

◄ **East Berlin, reunited with the west**
The River Spree flows into east Berlin near the avenue of Unter den Linden. From 1961 until 1989 the city of Berlin was divided by a wall manned by armed guards.

same currency. The land of Austria descends from the soaring peaks of the Alps to the flat lands of the Danube river valley. Austria once ruled a large empire which stretched eastward into Hungary and southward into Italy. Today Austria still plays an important part in Europe, making its living from tourism, farming, forestry, and manufacture. Austria too has a rich background in music and the arts.

German is spoken through most of the region, with a great variety of dialects. In German cities you may also hear Turkish and southern European languages being spoken, as people from other countries have come to seek work in Germany since the 1960s. In parts of Switzerland there are also speakers of French, Italian, and Romansh. Northern Germany and Switzerland are mostly Protestant, while southern Germany and Austria are mostly Roman Catholic.

▼ **Watching the world go by**
Cafés, shops, and hotels line the longest street in west Berlin. This is the stylish Kurfürstendamm, known for short as the "Ku'damm."

Bay of Biscay

Cape Ortegal
Cape Peñas

ANDORRA

La Coruña
El Ferrol
Carballo
Villalba
Oviedo
Gijón
Llanes
Santander
Bilbao
San Sebastián
Cape Finisterre
Fonsagrada
CANTABRIAN
MOUNTAINS
PYRENEES
Lugo
Reinosa
Vitoria
Pamplona
Santiago de Compostela
Sarria
Sil
Ebro
Arga
Gállego
Cinca
Lalin
Monforte de Lemos
León
Astorga
Osorno
Burgos
Logroño
Vigo
Orense
SIERRA CABRERA
Villada
Palencia
Soria
Saragossa
Ebro
Miño
Baltar
La Gudina
Esla
Caspe
Braga
Bragança
Valladolid
Duero
Jalón
S P A I N
Mogadouro
Zamora
Támega
Tuela
Vila Real
Medina del Campo
Segovia
SIERRA DE GUADARRAMA
Tajuña
Tajo
Morella
Porto
Douro
Tormes
Salamanca
Guadalajara
Alcalá de Henares
Teruel
Mijares
Lamego
PORTUGAL
Avila
Madrid
Cuenca
Castellón de la Plana
Aviero
Viseu
Cuidad Rodrigo
Bejar
SIERRA DE GREDOS
Turia
Sagunto
Guarda
Covilhã
Plasencia
Tajo
Aranjuez
Coimbra
Castelo Branco
Toledo
Requena
Valencia
Leiria
Tomar
Tagus
Trujillo
Cáceres
MONTES DE TOLEDO
Júcar
Alcira
Gulf of Valencia
Caldas da Rainha
Portalegre
Daimiel
Villarrobledo
Albacete
Santarém
Manzanares
Almansa
Lisbon
Don Benito
Ciudad Real
Alcoy
Badajoz
Guadiana
Alcaraz
Yecla
Évora
Almendralejo
Puertollano
Valdepeñas
Alicante
Elche
Setúbal
Ardila
Pozoblanco
SIERRA DE SEGURA
Segura
Orihuela
Azuaga
SIERRA MORENA
La Carolina
Moratalla
Murcia
Costa Blanca
Beja
Guadiana
Constantina
Córdoba
Linares
Cehegin
Cape Palos
Chança
Nerva
Guadalquivir
Jaén
Martos
Lorca
Cartagena
Lagos
Huelva
Seville
Puente Genil
Baza
Aguilas
Faro
Algarve
Costa de la Luz
Osuna
Guadix
Huércal Overa
Cape Saint Vincent
Gulf of Cadiz
Las Marismas
Morón de la Frontera
Antequera
Genil
Granada
Mulhacén 3,478m
Almería
Costa Blanca
Jerez de la Frontera
Ronda
SIERRA NEVADA
Málaga
Motril
Berja
Cape Gata
Cádiz
SIERRA DE RONDA
Marbella
Costa del Sol
M E D I T E R R A N E A N   S E A
Gibraltar (U.K.)
Algeciras
Strait of Gibraltar
PORTUGAL
Cueta (Spain)

Melilla (Spain)

SPAIN

THE IBERIAN PENINSULA

The Iberian peninsula is in southwestern Europe, jutting out like a great fist into the Atlantic Ocean. It is bordered to the north by the stormy Bay of Biscay and to the south by the Mediterranean Sea and the Balearic Islands. The region is occupied by Spain, Portugal, Andorra, and Gibraltar.

The Iberian Peninsula's north coast, green from high rainfall, rises to the Cantabrian mountains, while the snowy Pyrenees form a high barrier along the Spanish-French frontier. These mountains are the location of a tiny independent country called Andorra. Another snow-capped range, the Sierra Nevada, runs parallel with the peninsula's southern coast.

▶ **A corner of old Seville**
Seville is a beautiful old city in the Anadalucía region of Spain. The bell tower of its massive cathedral was once part of a Muslim mosque.

◀ **Earthenware pots**
Containers made of terra cotta can be seen all over the Mediterranean. These traditional designs are centuries old.

The Spanish capital, Madrid, lies right at the centre of the Iberian peninsula. Much of this inland region is taken up by an extremely dry, rocky plateau, the Meseta, which swelters in the heat of summer. Spain's southern coast sweeps down to the Strait of Gibraltar, just 8 miles from the mainland of Africa. The steep rock of Gibraltar, controlling the entrance to the Mediterranean Sea, is a British colony. The west of the Iberian peninsula takes in rocky, forested highlands, and the fertile plains of Portugal, crossed by great rivers. Lisbon, the Portuguese capital, lies on the north shore of the River Tagus.

Spain and Portugal are the two largest Iberian countries. Both have a rich history. They were conquered in the early Middle Ages by the Moors— Muslim Berbers and Arabs from North Africa, who left behind fine palaces and cities. Eventually the peninsula was reconquered by Christians from the north.

▲ *In the highlands of Portugal*
Vineyards cover the sunny slopes of Buçaco, to the north of Coimbra. Portugal produces many red and rosé wines.

▼ *Along the Costa del Sol*
Spain's Costa del Sol ("sunshine coast") is in the south. Nerja, a former fishing village, attracts many tourists.

Portugal and Spain led the European exploration of Africa and Asia, and went on to discover the "New World" of the Americas in the 1490s and 1500s. Spanish and Portuguese are still the chief languages of Central and South America. Both Spain and Portugal suffered rule by dictators for much of the twentieth century, but today both are democracies and members of the European Union.

Spain produces olives, citrus fruits, wines, and sherries, and has a large fishing fleet. It has reserves of iron ore and produces steel and motor vehicles. Portugal is one of western Europe's poorer countries. It produces wine and port, a strong sweet wine that takes its name from the city of

Oporto. Fishing villages line the Atlantic coast and cork is cut from the thick bark of a kind of oak tree.

Many tourists visit the Iberian peninsula, enjoying the small whitewashed villages, the historical towns, the great cathedrals, and the medieval castles. The warm beaches of the south, lined by high-rise hotels, are especially popular with vacationers from northern Europe.

The whole region is strongly Roman Catholic, and life in both Spain and Portugal is marked by colorful festivals marking saints' days. During Holy Week, the period before the Christian festival

▲ *From the days of the Moors*
The fabulous Mezquita in Córdoba, Spain, is a mosque from the Middle Ages, when the Muslim city was a great center of civilization.

of Easter, holy statues are carried through the streets.

Spain is famous for flamenco, a fiery combination of Gypsy guitar, wild singing, and strutting, stamping dance steps. Portugal has fado, a sadder, more plaintive style of folk song. Bullfighting is an ancient Spanish tradition, full of colorful ceremony but criticized as cruel by many foreign visitors.

◀ *Paella delight*
The best known Spanish dish is paella. Cooked in a heavy pan, it includes saffron rice, chicken or seafood, as well as garlic and vegetables.

IBERIAN PEOPLES

The Iberian peninsula is home to many different peoples, cultures and languages and this has led to conflict in some regions.

The Basques live in the far north and their homeland stretches westward from the city of Bilbao into France. Their language, Euskara, is not related to any other and may be the oldest in Europe.

The Galicians live along the rías or sea inlets of the northwest and they claim descent from the ancient Celts. Their language is called Gallego.

The Catalans live in the regions around the great cultural center of Barcelona, as well as in Andorra and across the border in France. The Catalan language is widely spoken.

MONACO

LIGURIAN
SEA

ITALY

SAN MARINO

ITALY

Corsica
(France)

VATICAN CITY

Strait of Bonifacio

Asinara

Sardinia

MALTA

LIPARI
ISLANDS

Sicily

MALTA CHAN

MALTA

ITALY AND ITS NEIGHBORS

Italy occupies a long peninsula in the Mediterranean Sea. It takes in the large islands of Sardinia and Sicily and also surrounds two patches of independent territory, Vatican City and San Marino. Malta is an island nation lying to the south.

Shaped like a high-heeled boot, Italy divides the blue waters of the Mediterranean into the Ligurian and Tyrrhenian Seas in the west and the Adriatic Sea in the east.

The north of Italy descends from the high, snowy peaks and sparkling lakes of the Alps to wide, fertile plains around the River Po. The wealthiest industrial cities, such as Milan and Bologna, are located in the north.

A long chain of mountains, the Appenines, run down the spine of Italy and takes in the little state of San Marino. The mountains are wooded and a home to a rich vaiety of wildlife, including rare gray wolves. The mountains are flanked by the vineyards of

▲ *Streets made of water*
A maze of canals serve as streets in Venice, one of Europe's most beautiful cities. Boats are used for transportation.

Tuscany and the rich farmland around the Bay of Naples. In the far south are hot, dry plains, rocks and scrub. This is the poorest part of Italy. Southern Italy and its islands form one of the world's danger zones for earthquakes. Famously violent volcanoes

◄ On the Gulf of Salerno
The pretty town of Positano climbs steeply from blue seas. Tourist resorts in this region also include Amalfi and the island of Capri.

world. Factories produce cars, textiles and leather goods. Milan is famous for fashion, and Venice for glass-making.

Modern Italy has only been united since 1861, but in ancient times Rome was the capital of a vast empire which stretched across western Europe, southwest Asia and North Africa. During the 1400s and 1500s cities such as Florence saw a great flowering of scholarship and the arts, known as the Renaissance ("rebirth"). Few other countries can boast so many well-preserved historical buildings and works of art. Tourists from all over the world visit Italy to see its ancient sites.

include Vesuvius, near Naples, and Etna, on Sicily.

The Italian capital is the ancient city of Rome, on the River Tiber. One district of Rome, Vatican City, is the world's smallest independent state, serving as headquarters for the Roman Catholic Church and its Popes.

Italy was a founder member of what is now the European Union. Olives and grapes grow well in its sunny climate and Italy is the largest wine producer in the

Italian, based on the ancient Latin language, is spoken throughout Italy,

◄ St. Peter's Square
This part of Vatican City, in the center of Rome, is where crowds of Christians often gather to be blessed by the Pope.

► The Leaning Tower of Pisa
This medieval bell tower may be seen in Pisa. Built on unstable ground, it now leans over from the vertical by about 16 feet.

but in border regions you may hear other languages, such as French, German, or Slovenian. The Ladin language is spoken in the Dolomite mountains of the northeast, and the people of Sardinia speak their own ancient dialect of Italian.

Italians are nearly all Roman Catholics. Many are great lovers of opera and movies and supporters of soccer. The population as a whole numbers about 57.4 million. In the last 150 years many Italians have left their homeland in search of work overseas, and there are large Italian communities in Northern Europe, the United States of America, and Australia.

To the south of Sicily, toward the coast of North Africa, is the chain of islands that make up Malta. Its capital is the seaport of Valletta. Malta was a British colony from 1814 until 1964, when it became independent. The population of over 360,000 lives on the islands of Malta, Gozo, and Comino. The Maltese have their own language, which has been influenced by dialects of Italian and Arabic. The chief industries are tourism, ship building, and repair.

▲ *Spaghetti Bolognese*
Spaghetti is a kind of pasta. Here it is served with a meat and tomato sauce, invented in the city of Bologna.

◄ *Into the Grand Canal*
The Customs House, built in 1672, dominates this section of Venice's Grand Canal. Many artists have painted this scene over the centuries.

ESTONIA

LITHUANIA

▲ *Traditional sounds*
*The zither is a flat,
stringed instrument which
has been played by folk
musicians in Central
Europe for centuries.*

LATVIA

POLAND

SLOVAKIA

**CZECH
REPUBLIC**

HUNGARY

ESTONIA

Kohtla-Järve
Tallinn
Hiumaa
Lake Peipus
Saaremaa
Parnu
Tartu
Munamagi ▲
RUSSIA

Gulf of Riga
LATVIA
Ventspils
Jurmala
Gaizina ▲
Saldus
Riga
Liepaja
Jelgava
Daugavpils
Siauliai
Panevezys
Utena
Klaipeda
LITHUANIA
Ukmerge
Nemunas (Neman)
Kaunas
Vilnius
**Kaliningrad
(RUSSIA)**
Gulf of Gdansk
Gdynia
Kaliningrad
BELARUS
Gdansk
Kolobrzeg
Elblag
Olsztyn
Szczecin
N O R T H   E U R O P E A N   P L A I N
Bydgoscz
Bialystock
Gorzow Wielkopolski
Torun
Poznan
Plock
Kalisz
Warsaw
P O L A N D
Glogow
Lodz
Odra (Oder)
Radom
Lublin
Wroclaw
Kielce
Chelm
Walbrzych
Czestochowa
SUDETES MOUNTAINS
Bytom
UKRAINE
Karlovy Vary
Prague
Katowice
Krakow
Rzeszow
Plzen
Pardubice
Tychy
Tarnow
BOHEMIA
**C Z E C H
R E P U B L I C**
Ostrava
Bielsko-Biala
Olomouc
CARPATHIAN MOUNTAINS
MORAVIA
Cesky Budejovice
Zilina
Rysy Peak
Presov
Brno
Trencin
Kosice
AUSTRIA
**S L O V A K
R E P U B L I C**
Miskolc
Nytra
Bratislava
Mt. Kekes ▲
Debrecen
Danube
Györ
Budapest
Tatabanya
Szombathely
H U N G A R Y
Koros
ROMANIA
Lake Balaton
Tisza
Bekescsaba
Kaposvar
Szeged
Pécs
CROATIA
YUGOSLAVIA
GERMANY

CENTRAL EUROPE

Three small countries cluster around the eastern shores of the Baltic Sea—Estonia, Latvia, and Lithuania. Poland lies on the Baltic's southern shore, between Germany and Eastern Europe. Across the mountains of southern Poland lie the Czech and Slovak Republics and Hungary, on the River Danube.

The Baltic states of Estonia, Latvia, and Lithuania are made up of forests and lakes, farmland and industrial cities. For much of their history they have been ruled by their larger neighbors, and were part of the Soviet Union (today's Russian Federation) from

▲ *Dolls in the market*
Sets of wooden dolls which fit one into the other, in the Russian style, are popular tourist souvenirs.

1940 until 1991. During this period many Russians settled in the region. However, each of the Baltic states managed to keep its own language and culture.

Poland is a large country and has also known invasions and foreign rule through much of its history. Like the countries to the south, Poland remained under strict Soviet influence from the late 1940s until 1989. The Poles, a Slavic people, also kept alive a pride in their country's traditions.

The lands near Poland's Baltic coast are dotted with lakes. The north of the country is flat, forested land,

◄ *The last of the bisons*
The European bison, or wisent, was rescued from the brink of extinction in the 1950s and can be seen today in Poland's Bialowieza forest.

▼ *Tasty exports*
Barrels at the brewery waiting for export. The Czech republic produces beers which are now on sale throughout the world.

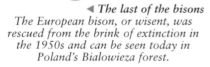

part of the great plain that stretches from eastern Germany into Russia. It is cold and snowy in winter, but warm in summer. In southern Poland the land rises to highlands and the jagged peaks of the Tatra mountains. Poland has reserves of coal and produces steel and heavy machinery. Its farmlands produce wheat, potatoes, and beets. Its most famous export is vodka, a fiery liquor.

Slovakia and the Czech Republic were a single country until 1993. Slovakia is a land of high mountains dropping to fertile farmland around the River Danube, which forms its southeastern border. When the two countries divided, most of the industries lay on the Czech side of the border. The Czech Republic, with its capital at Prague, produces beer, glass, ceramics, steel, and machinery. The country

▲ **Old-time Prague**
This old clock may be seen in Prague, capital of the Czech Republic. This fine city on the River Vltava attracts many tourists.

▶ **Waterchess in the baths**
Here is the perfect way to enjoy the beneficial spa waters which are a normal part of Hungarian life.

SOUNDS OF CENTRAL EUROPE
The balalaika is a musical instrument with a triangular body and a long neck like a guitar. Its jangling sounds are popular in Central Europe, Russia and the Balkans. The folk music of the region also makes use of fiddles. It has been influenced in places by Gypsy dance music and has in turn influenced some classical composers.

► *Soldiers on Parade* Lithuanian troops march past during the Independence Day celebrations. Lithuania finally won full independence in 1991.

is bordered by mountains and, in the east, by the Bohemian Forest. Bohemia was the name of the kingdom that grew up here in the Middle Ages.

The Czechs and Slovaks are both Slavic peoples, but the Hungarians are Magyars, a people who invaded and settled the region about 1,200 years ago. Hungary is a country of wide open plains and low mountains. Its fertile farmland produces fruits, grains and grapes for making strong red wine. Its beautiful capital, Budapest, is on the River Danube. Before 1918 Hungary and its neighbors were joined with Austria in a large Central European empire.

Central Europe has also been settled by other peoples over the ages, including the Roma (Gypsies) and the Jews. Central Europe is largely Roman Catholic in faith, with Protestant and Russian Orthodox groups around the Baltic.

◄ *Five horsepower* This skilled horseman controls five lively horses at a Herdsman and Horseman Show in Kiskunsagi National Park, Hungary.

43

ROMANIA

BULGARIA

SLOVENIA

CROATIA

UKRAINE

Satu Mare
Baia Mare
Botosani
Iasi
MOLDOVA

AUSTRIA
Maribor
Oradea
Cluj-Napoca
Somes
Mures
Bacau
MOLDAVIAN CARPATHIANS
Siret

Triglav
Ljubljana
Sava
Koprivnica
HUNGARY
Arad
Mures
Tirgu Mures
Alba Iulia
ROMANIA

SLOVENIA
Zagreb
Drava
Subotica
Timisoara
Deva
Sibiu
Brasov
Galati

Rijeka
Kupa
Prijedor
Sava
Osijek
VOJVODINA
Resita
Moldoveanu
TRANSYLVANIAN ALPS
Braila

Pula
Bihac
Banja Luka
Novi Sad
Belgrade
Jiu
Ploiesti
DOBRUJA

Cres
Gospic
BOSNIA -
HERZEGOVINA
Brcko
Pitesti

Losinj
Zadar
Dugi I.
Livno
Zenica
Tuzla
Sabac
Smederevo
Negotin
Craiova
Bucharest
Constanta

Sibenik
DINARIC ALPS
Sarajevo
Srebrenica
Valjevo
Kragujevac
Vidin
Dunarea (Danube)
Ruse
Dobrich

Split
Livno
Mostar
Drina
Cacak
Morava
Mikhaylovgrad
Iskur
Pleven
Lovech
Turgovishte
Shumen
Balchik
Varna

Hvar
Brac
Vis
Korcula
Krusevac
SERBIA
Nis
Vratsa
BALKAN MOUNTAINS
Kazanluk
Kamchiya

Lastovo
Mljet
Dubrovnik
Novi Pazar
MONTENEGRO
Leskovac
Sofia
Sliven
Burgas

Podgorica
Pec
Pristina
KOSOVO
Pernik
BULGARIA
Tundzha
Yambol

Lake Scutari
Urosevac
Musala Peak
Pasardzhik
Stara Zagora

Shkoder
Drin
Mt Korabit
Tetovo
Skopje
Plovdiv
Khaskovo

Gulf
Durres
Tirane
Prilep
MACEDONIA
Struma
Var dar
PIRIN MTS
RHODOPE MOUNTAINS
Smolyan
Orestiás
Komotini

Elbasan
Lake Ohrid
Bitola
Palikastron
Drama
Xanthi
Alexandroúpolis

Vlore
ALBANIA
Edhessa
Kilkís
Serrai
Kaválla
Thasos
Samothrace

Gjirokaster
Ptolemais
Náousa
Thessaloniki
Samothrace

Aliákmon
Mt Olympus
Mt Athos
Límnos

GREECE

Kérkira
Corfu
Párga
Ioánnina
Trikkala
Lárisa
Vólos
Skiathos
Skíros
Lesbos
Mitilíni

Arta
PINDUS MTS
Kardhítsa
Lamia
Skópelos
Euboea
AEGEAN

Pálairos
Parnassus
Kími
SEA
Chios

Leukas
Astakós
Agrinion
Khalkís

Cephalonia
Ithaca
Pátrai
Mégara
Marathon
Andros
Sámos

IONIAN
SEA
Amaliás
Lambia
Corinth
Piraeus
Athens
Ikaría

Zante
Alfios
Argos
Láyrion
Kea
Tinos
Mikonos
Pátmos

Pírgos
Tripolis
Návplion
Galatás
Kíthnos
Síros
Páros
Léros

PELOPONNESUS
Sparta
Serifos
Náxos
Kálimnos

Kalamáta
Sífnos
Ios
Cos

Areópolis
Neápolis
Milos
Thira
Astipálaia
Tílos
Rho

Cythera
Rhodes
Lind

SEA OF CRETE
Kárpathos

Khaniá

Réthimnon
Iráklion
Mt Ida
Crete

MACEDONIA

BOSNIA-
HERZEGOVINA

ALBANIA

GREECE

THE BALKANS

The states of southern Central Europe are known as the Balkans. They take their name from the Balkan peninsula, a broad wedge of land that stretches south into the Mediterranean Sea. The Balkans include Romania, Bulgaria, Albania, Greece, and the lands formerly grouped together as Yugoslavia.

The warm, blue waters around the Balkan coast form the Adriatic, Ionian, Aegean, and Black Seas. The region is largely mountainous, with hot, dry summers. Winters are severe in the north of the region, but generally mild in the south. Violent earthquakes are common.

The Balkan countries produce fruit, wines and liquors, wheat, dairy products such as yogurt and cheese, olives, sunflowers, and tobacco. Many parts of the region are poor. All have experienced long centuries of war, invasion and occupation. Peoples of the Balkans include Southern Slavs (such as Serbs, Croats, Slovenes, and Montenegrins), Albanians, Greeks, Bulgars, Turks, Roma (Gypsies), and Romanians. Religions include both Roman Catholic and Eastern Orthodox Christianity as well as Islam.

The northwest of the region is a patchwork of these peoples, each with their distinctive cultures, languages and beliefs. In the 1990s it exploded into bitter fighting and racial violence as the large nation of

▼ *Agricultural worker, Romania*
This lady wears the traditional headwear of scarf and straw hat to protect her from all weathers as she works on the land.

▼ *Pulled by oxen*
In the village of Szeg these Romanian farmers still use oxen to pull their hay wagons at harvest time.

Yugoslavia broke up into separate independent states. These took the names of Slovenia, Croatia, Yugoslavia (Serbia and Montenegro), and Macedonia (which is also the name of the northernmost province of Greece). The tourist industry along the northern Adriatic coast came to an end.

From 1946 until 1985 the small country of Albania, with its capital at Tiranë, was led by a communist named Enver Hoxha. He kept the country isolated from the rest of Europe. After Hoxha's death Albania moved away from communist government. It suffered great poverty and in the 1990s collapsed into political unrest and civil war.

The northeast of the Balkan peninsula is occupied by Bulgaria, a land of fertile farmland to the south of the River Danube, crossed by the Balkan and Rhodope mountain chains. Its northern neighbor is Romania, lying around the forested Carpathian mountain range and the Transylvanian Alps. On the Black Sea coast, the River Danube splits into separate waterways and forms a marshy delta region. The recent history of Romania has included the violent overthrow of the government in 1989.

The Balkan peninsula narrows to the south. Greece occupies the southern part of the mainland, which breaks up into the large headland of the Peloponnese and many scattered island chains. The largest island,

◀ **Croatian costume**
These folk musicians at Vrobovec in Croatia wear traditional costume. Croatian independence was recognized by the European Union in 1992.

◀ **Walking home after church**
These families are walking home after church, at Szeg in Romania. Most Romanians follow the Romanian Orthodox faith. Other Christian worshippers include Protestants, Uniates (Greek Catholics), and Roman Catholics.

◄ **The islands of Greece**
*Thíra, also known as Santorini,
is a popular tourist island to the
north of Crete. More than 3,600 years
ago it was the site of a massive volcanic
eruption.*

▼ **The Corinth Canal**
*In 1893 the narrow strip of land
joining the Peloponnese to the Greek
mainland near Corinth was severed by
a sheer, deep shipping canal.*

mountainous Crete, marks the southern limits of Greek territory. Greece has many small, whitewashed villages and beautiful beaches attracting visitors from all over the world. It also has large industrial centers and seaports. Greece is a member of the European Union. Although many of its people are still poor farmers and fishermen, in recent years tourism has helped Greece to become wealthier than the other Balkan countries. There are large Greek-speaking communities overseas, especially in Cyprus, the United States and Australia.

WHO ARE THE BULGARIANS?
In Bulgaria, the traditional costume may still be worn for regional festivals or for folk dancing. Heritage and tradition are being emphasized in a bid to attract tourists. Bulgarian culture has many influences, from Ancient Thracian to Macedonian, Slavic, Bulgar, Turkish, and Roma (Gypsy).

Greece was the centre of Europe's first great civilizations, between 4,000 and 2,000 years ago. It was here that democracy—meaning "rule by the people" was first tried out. The ancient rock of the Acropolis, with its splendid temple, the Parthenon, still towers above the Greek capital, Athens. The ancient Greeks were great thinkers, poets, dramatists, sculptors, and warriors. Under Alexander the Great (356-323BC) they conquered lands from Egypt to India, but were eventually defeated by the Romans.

47

RUSSIA AND ITS NEIGHBOURS

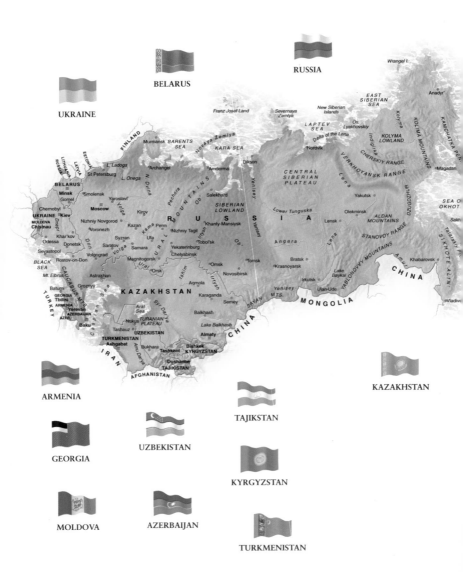

RUSSIA

BELARUS

UKRAINE

ARMENIA

GEORGIA

MOLDOVA

UZBEKISTAN

AZERBAIJAN

TAJIKSTAN

KYRGYZSTAN

TURKMENISTAN

KAZAKHSTAN

RUSSIA AND ITS NEIGHBORS

The Russian Federation is the biggest country in the world, stretching from eastern Europe right across Asia to the Pacific Ocean. Around it are a number of smaller countries. Belarus, Ukraine, and Moldova lie to the west. Georgia, Armenia and Azerbaijan lie to the southwest. Due south are the Central Asian states of Turkmenistan, Uzbekistan, and Kazakhstan.

For most of the last 100 years this region was dominated by one huge country, called the USSR or Soviet Union. That nation was formed in the years after November 1917, when communist revolutionaries ("Bolsheviks") seized power from the emperors, or czars, who had ruled Russia since the 1500s.

Communist rule ended in 1991 and many of the regions around the former Soviet borders then broke away to become independent countries—although most remained allies within a grouping called the Commonwealth of Independent States (CIS).

The remaining part of the former Soviet Union was renamed the "Russian Federation." The term "Russia" really only refers to one part of that federation, but is often used as a short form for the whole country. In the 1990s there was conflict when other parts of the federation, such as Chechnya, tried to break away.

The Russian Federation is still by far the largest country in the world, stretching across two continents and eight time zones. A journey from Moscow to the Pacific coast, on the famous Trans-Siberian Railroad, takes seven days.

The Russian capital is Moscow, a sprawling city of about 9

▼ *Siberian farmer*
This farmer works in extreme conditions. Winters in Siberia are severe with temperatures falling as low as -94°F (-70°C).

◄ *The Moscow metro*
Travelers crowd on to a Moscow subway station. The capital's Metro, built in the early days of communism, is decorated in a grand old-fashioned style.

million people. At its center is the wide open space of Red Square and the walls of the Kremlin. This ancient fortress, which became the center of government power in the old Soviet Union, contains fine old churches with gleaming domes. To the north is the former capital of St. Petersburg, a splendid city founded by a Czar Peter the Great in 1703.

Northern Russia is a land of tundra, where deep-frozen soil borders the Arctic Ocean. To the south is the great belt of forest known as taiga, whose spruce

trees are heavy with snow during the long, bitter winters. However, summers can be warm and sunny. To the south are the steppe grasslands, the shores of the Black Sea and the high mountains of the Caucasus. The Ural range, running from north to south, marks the border between European and Asian Russia.

Russia is rich in minerals and timber. Its industries were developed in a hurry during the Soviet years, but at great cost to the Russian people and the environment. Russia is still an economic giant, producing machinery, textiles, chemicals, and vehicles and it still launches spacecraft. However, recent years have seen huge economic problems, rising crime and political unrest.

▼ *Market stalls in Yerevan*
Local produce is laid out at an indoor market in Yerevan. The countryside around the Armenian capital produces citrus fruits, grapes, figs, olives, and almonds.

▼ *A federation of peoples*
More than 150 different peoples live in the Russian Federation, many with their own languages, traditions, and costumes, still worn for special festivals or folk dances.

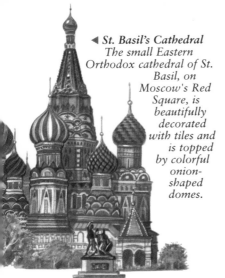

◀ *St. Basil's Cathedral*
The small Eastern Orthodox cathedral of St. Basil, on Moscow's Red Square, is beautifully decorated with tiles and is topped by colorful onion-shaped domes.

lands are industrialized, with the rich black soil of the Ukrainian steppes providing a large yield of wheat. In the Caucasus region, sunny Georgia and Armenia grow citrus fruits and grapes.

The lands around the Caspian and Aral Seas include dusty, thin grasslands grazed by sheep and goats, mountains, and deserts. Crops include cotton and wheat. Carpetmaking is a traditional craft skill of the region. There are large reserves of oil and natural gas, which will have a great impact on the region's economy and development in the twenty-first century.

The western CIS countries, home to Slavs, Georgians, and Armenians, have a long Christian tradition, but the Turkic and Mongol peoples of the eastern countries are mostly Muslims.

Eighty percent of the Russian Federation's population of 147,300,000 are Russians (a Slavic people), but the rest belong to many other ethnic groups which also live in the country. The Eastern Orthodox Church, no friend of the Bolsheviks, has today regained some of the power it enjoyed under the czars.

Popular sports in Russia include soccer, ice hockey, track and field, and ice skating. Russia has produced many of the greatest musical composers in history, such as Piotr Ilyich Tchaikovsky (1840-1893), as well as wonderful ballet companies such as the Bolshoi and Kirov. Famous Russian writers include Leo Tolstoy, who wrote *War and Peace* in 1863-1869.

Since independence, some of the other CIS countries have shared many of the same problems as Russia, including civil war, political unrest, and organized crime. The western CIS

TO THE UNKNOWN SOLDIER
Just by the Kremlin, a flame burns in memory of the "unknown soldier"—any one of the soldiers who died in defence of "Mother Russia." When Russia was invaded by the Germans in the 1940s, the people endured very great hardship. Their bravery was backed by a natural ally—the harsh Russian winter, which had also helped to defeat French invaders in 1811.

GREENLAND

LINCOLN
SEA

ARCTIC
OCEAN

Ellesmere
Island

GREENLAND

Melville Island

Devon Island

BAFFIN BAY

BEAUFORT
SEA

Banks Island

Prince
of Wales
Island

Victoria Island

Baffin Island

Davis Strait

ALASKA (U.S.A.)

Dawson

Norman Wells

Great Bear
Lake

FOXE BASIN

LABRADOR
SEA

Mt. Logan

YUKON
TERRITORY

Whitehorse

MACKENZIE MOUNTAINS

NORTHWEST TERRITORIES

Southampton
Island

Hudson Strait

Mackenzie

Liard

HORN
MOUNTAINS

Yellowknife

Great Slave Lake

Fort Resolution

Fort Smith

Dubawnt
Lake

Coats Island

Mansel Island

Ungava
Peninsula

Feuilles

CARIBOU
MOUNTAINS

Lake
Athabasca

HUDSON BAY

Prince Rupert

Prince George

COAST MOUNTAINS

BRITISH
COLUMBIA

Peace

CANADA

Reindeer
Lake

Churchill

Nelson

Churchill

Belcher Islands

La Grande Rivière

QUEEN
CHARLOTTE
ISLANDS

ROCKY MOUNTAINS

Peace River

ALBERTA

Edmonton

MANITOBA

Severn

JAMES
BAY

Akimiski
Island

OTISH
MOUNTAINS

Peribonca

Vancouver
Island

Kamloops

Red Deer

N. Saskatchewan

Prince Albert

Lake
Winnipegosis

Lake
Winnipeg

Albany

St.

Victoria

Vancouver

Medicine Hat

Calgary

Saskatoon

SASKATCHEWAN

ONTARIO

QUEBEC

Quebec

Fre

S. Saskatchewan

Regina

Lake
Manitoba

Lake Nipigon

Montreal

UNITED STATES OF AMERICA

Winnipeg

Thunder Bay

Lake Superior

Ottawa

Georgian Bay

Lake Huron

Toronto

Lake Ontario

Hamilton

Niagara Falls

Windsor

Lake Erie

CANADA

GREENLAND AND CANADA

The North American Arctic is a deep-frozen land of ice and rock, of sea inlets and remote islands. It includes Greenland and northern Canada. Canada extends southward to the United States border. It is bounded in the west by the Pacific Ocean and the state of Alaska, and in the east by the Atlantic Ocean.

▶ *Across the ice*
The traditional means of transportation in the Arctic was the dogsled. Sleds are still used, although today most people use a snowmobile instead.

Separated from the North American mainland by the Davis Strait, Greenland (or Kallaalit Nunaat) is a territory of Denmark, but now has complete home rule. This is the world's biggest island, but inland most of the land is buried under permanent ice. The population lives around the coast and numbers only about 55,000. Most are Inuit (Eskimo), with a minority of Scandinavian or mixed descent. The chief industries are fishery and fish-processing. There are plans to prospect for minerals and to develop tourism.

Another European possession in the North American continent is the little island territory of St. Pierre and Miquelon, which is ruled by France.

Canada is the second largest country in the world, and yet it is home to only 30 million people. Most Canadians live in the big, bustling cities of the far south, such as Montréal, Toronto, and, in the far west, Vancouver. The capital and home of the Canadian parliament is the smaller city of Ottawa, in southeastern Ontario.

Canada's southeastern provinces include Newfoundland and Labrador, and the "Maritimes" (Nova Scotia, New Brunswick, and Prince Edward Island). Canada's fishing grounds on the foggy North Atlantic were once the world's richest, but have declined disastrously in recent years.

The huge southern provinces of Québec and Ontario take in the St. Lawrence River and its Seaway, an engineered link which makes it possible for

◄ *Lumber for the sawmills*
Great rafts of felled tree trunks are floated down the Coulonge, a tributary of the Ottawa River in southwest Québec province.

► *Toronto skyline*
Toronto, on Lake Ontario, is Canada's biggest city, with a population of 3,893,000. Its skyline is dominated by the 1,814 foot CN Tower.

ocean going ships to reach the big cities of the Great Lakes. In the north these provinces border Hudson Bay, along a vast rim of ancient rock called the Canadian Shield. The prairies, natural grasslands which extend across the United States border, are given over to wheat and cattle farming. Prairie provinces include Manitoba, Saskatchewan, and Alberta. Beyond the snowy peaks of the Rocky Mountains, the mild, moist climate of British Columbia supports large areas of evergreen forest.

The severe climate makes it hard for people to live in the northern wilderness, which stretches across Yukon Territory, Northwest Territories (NWT), and Nunavut, the vast Inuit homeland which will break away from NWT in 1999. Here, a broad belt of spruce forest gives way to bare, deep frozen soil called tundra.

Canada's wilderness areas are home to polar bears and seals, caribou, moose, beavers, and loons. They also have valuable resources, providing timber, hydroelectric power and minerals, including oil. Most Canadians enjoy a high standard of living. Since 1994 Canada has been a member of the North American Free Trade Agreement (NAFTA).

The original Canadians crossed into North America from Asia long ago, when the two continents were joined by land. They were ancestors of the peoples now known in the United States as Native Americans and in Canada as First Peoples. They were followed by the Inuit people of the Arctic. Today these two groups make up only four percent of Canada's population. Many have kept their languages and traditions alive, but have also suffered from poverty and from the development of their

► *As far as the eye can see*
A field of golden wheat stretches to the horizon in the prairie province of Saskatchewan — one of the world's great grain-producing regions, or "breadbaskets".

traditional hunting grounds and fisheries.

In the 1500s eastern Canada was explored and settled by French and British fur traders and fishermen. In the 1700s the French and British battled to control Canada, and it ended up as a dominion, or self-ruling nation, within the British empire. Today, about 40 percent of Canadians are descended from peoples of the British Isles, especially Scots. People of French descent make up 27 percent, and there are also many other minorities, including Ukrainians, Germans, Scandinavians, Chinese, Vietnamese, and Afro-Caribbeans.

Canada has two official languages, French and English, and over the last 35 years many people in the French-speaking province of Québec have campaigned to become separate from the rest of Canada. Most Canadians are

---

MAPLE LEAF COUNTRY
The emblem of Canada is the leaf of the maple tree, which appears on the national flag. Various types of maple grow in Canada. Sugar maples are grown in Ontario, Québec, and New Brunswick. The sweet, sticky sap is collected and boiled to make natural maple syrup or sirop d'érable — an invention of the Native American peoples of this region. It is delicious served with pancakes or ice cream.

Christians. French-speakers are mostly Roman Catholic and English-speakers are mostly Protestant.

Because most Canadian cities are so near the USA, American influences on the way of life have been very strong. Even so, Canadians like to do things in their own way and take pride in their differences. Canada has made an international name for itself in sports such as ice hockey, in literature, films, and popular music.

◀ *Ice hockey*
Ice hockey was first played in Canada, and is still hugely popular. Major teams include the Montréal Canadiens and the Toronto Maple Leafs.

▲ *In the blue Canadian Rockies*
A brimming lake, forests of spruce and tamarack (a kind of larch), and snowy peaks make up the classic landscape of Alberta.

ALASKA (U.S.A.)

▶ **National Bird**
The magnificent Bald
Eagle is the emblem of
the United States.

**THE UNITED STATES
OF AMERICA**

▶ **Wrestling a steer**
Rodeos are a chance to
show off ranching skills.
The cowboys and
pioneers of the 1800s are
still heroes to many
Americans.

UNITED STATES OF AMERICA

The United States of America (USA) make up a huge country that straddles eight time zones. It extends across the North American continent from the Pacific to the Atlantic Oceans, from Canada south to Mexico. It includes great cities which light up the night sky, as well as large areas of remote wilderness and virgin forest.

The northeastern part of the United States has an even climate, although winter snowfall can be heavy and summers can be very warm. Inland from the rocks and stormy shores of the Atlantic coast are the woodlands of New England, which turn to every shade of red and gold in the autumn. Here there are broad rivers and neat little towns dating back to the days of the early European settlers, and also the historic city of Boston, Massachusetts. In the far north the Great Lakes mark the border with Canada. On this border are the spectacular Niagara Falls, a major tourist attraction which also provides valuable hydroelectric power. The Appalachian mountain ranges run for 1,488 miles from north to south, through the eastern United States.

The northeastern states include centers of industry and mining, and large cities with gleaming skyscrapers, sprawling suburbs, road, and rail networks. New York City, centred on the island of Manhattan, is the business capital of the USA and also a lively center of arts and entertainment. To many people, New York City is a symbol of America—fast-moving and energetic, a melting pot of different peoples and cultures. The northern city of Detroit is a centre of the motor industry, and Chicago, on the shores of Lake Michigan, is another bustling city of skyscrapers, a center of business and manufacture.

Traveling south from the Delaware River and the great city of Philadelphia, you come to the Potomac River and the federal District of Columbia (DC), the site of Washington,

◄ **Welcome to Boston!**
Boston, the state capital of Massachussets, has a large population of Italian and Irish Americans. It is the chief commercial and industrial centre of New England.

capital city of the United States. Approaching the American South, you pass into warmer country where tobacco and cotton are grown in the red earth. The long peninsula of Florida extends southwards into the Caribbean Sea, fringed by sandy islands called keys. Along the Gulf coast the climate is hot and very humid, with creeks known as bayous and tangled swamps which are home to alligators. Hurricanes are common in late summer and autumn. New Orleans, the home of jazz, has many picturesque old buildings with wrought-iron verandahs. It lies 105 miles above the mouth of the Mississippi River, which together with the mighty Missouri drains the centre of the continent. Texas is a huge state bordering Mexico along the Rio Grande. Dry and dusty, it makes its living from cattle ranching and oil.

Prairies once covered the great plains of the Midwest, the home of vast herds of bison or buffalo.

▲ **Baseball country**
Baseball is an all-American invention. It was invented by Abner Doubleday and became popular in the 1800s.

▼ **Grand Canyon, Arizona**
A glowing panorama stretches out from the north rim of the Grand Canyon. The canyon was shaped by the waters of the Colorado River.

Today the grasslands are largely given over to farming vegetable crops, corn, and wheat, or to cattle ranching. Barren, stony "badlands" rise toward the rugged Rocky Mountain ranges, which form the backbone of the USA as they stretch from the Canadian border south to Mexico.

Southward and westward again there are large areas of burning desert, salt flats, and canyons, where over the ages the rocks have been worn into fantastic shapes by wind and water. In places, Arizona's spectacular Grand Canyon is 14 miles wide and 1.2 miles deep.

Badwater, in Calfornia's harsh Death Valley, is the lowest point in the United States, 282 feet below sea level.

The Sierra,

Cascade, and Coast ranges run parallel with the beautiful Pacific coast. The warm beaches, pines and gigantic redwood trees of California stretch northwards to the rainy and cool ferny forests of Oregon and Washington State. Irrigation has made it possible to farm large areas of California, which produce citrus fruits and grape vines. Major cities of the west include Los Angeles, which takes in the world-famous film studios of Hollywood, beautiful San Francisco, set on a wide bay which can be warm and sparkling blue or shrouded in cool sea fog, and the busy northern port of Seattle.

The United States has a northern outpost in oil-rich Alaska, its largest state. Alaska

▲ *Modern cityscapes*
Dallas, Texas, is a business center for the oil and cotton trade. Skyscrapers were invented in the United States, and many cities are dominated by modern architecture.

was purchased from Russia in 1867. Bordered by Canada, the Alaskan wilderness stretches into the remote Arctic, a deep frozen land of mountains and tundra. Its islands are inhabited by large grizzly bears and its waters by schools of migrating whales. Mount McKinley, at 20,316 feet, is the highest point not just in the United States, but in all of North America. Far to the west, in the Pacific Ocean, the Hawaiian Islands are also part of the USA. Tourists come here to enjoy the warm climate, surf, and the islands' spectacular volcanoes.

The United States also governs or has special links with various other territories, such as American Samoa, the Northern Marianas and the Midway Islands in the Pacific Ocean, and Puerto Rico and the US Virgin Islands in the Caribbean.

Native American peoples were the first to settle North America, migrating from Asia possibly as

▲ *Wide open spaces*
A car follows a lonely road through Monument Valley, on the Arizona-Utah border—the homeland of the Navajo people.

early as 30,000 years ago. From the 1500s onward Native American lands were seized and settled by colonists from Europe. In 1776 the British colonies in the east declared their independence, and during the 1800s their new country, the United States of America, grew rapidly as it gained territory from France, Mexico and Russia. Today, in addition to the small Native American population, there are Americans whose ancestors originally came from Britain, Ireland, Italy, France, Germany, the Netherlands and Poland.

JAMBALAYA!
Rice, seafood, green peppers, and hot spices make up this delicious dish from steamy New Orleans, in Louisiana. The inhabitants of this city include many people of French and African descent, and these influences are reflected in its cooking.

There are African Americans, whose ancestors were brought to America to work as slaves. There are Jews, Armenians, Spanish, Chinese, Cubans, Hawaiians, Vietnamese, and Koreans. All are citizens of the United States.

The nation today is a federation of 50 states, which have the power to pass many of their own laws. The federal seat of government is at the capital, Washington, DC. Here is the Congress, made up of a Senate and a House of Representatives, and the White House, the home of the US Presidents.

▶ *Surf's up!*
Surfing is popular in California and in the state of Hawaii, in the Pacific. It is said that the Polynesian inhabitants of Hawaii invented the sport long ago.

The American economy is the most powerful in the world and its influences are felt globally. The country is rich in minerals, including oil, coal and iron ore. American companies produce computers and software, aircraft, cars, and processed foods and there are also many large banks and finance companies. The United States is the leader in space exploration and technology. Films and television programmes made in Hollywood have made the American way of life very influential around the world. American hamburgers and soft drinks are now bought in many other countries. Popular sports include football, baseball, and basketball.

The USA has close economic links with its neighbors, Canada and Mexico, through the North American Free Trade Agreement (NAFTA) of 1994. It is also a member of many other international groupings, such as the Organization of American States (OAS) and the North Atlantic Treaty Organization (NATO), a military alliance that links it with Western and Central Europe.

KAUAI

Lihue

Kauai Channel

OAHU

Honolulu

MOLOKAI

Wailuku

LANAI

MAUI

Lanai City

KAHOOLAWE

Alenuihaha Channel

Mauna Kea

HAWAII

Hilo

Mauna Loa

BAHAMAS

BELIZE

JAMAICA

HAITI

ANTIGUA AND
BARBUDA

HONDURAS

PUERTO RICO

DOMINICA

PANAMA

CUBA

Tijuana Mexicali
Ensenada

UNITED STATES OF AMERICA

Ciudad Juárez

Cedros I.

Hermosillo

Chihuahua

Rio Grande

Rio Bravo del Norte

BAHAMAS

B A H A M A S

Nassau

Turks &
Caicos
Islands (U.

Andros I.

Torreón

La Paz

Culiacán

Saltillo

Durango

Monterrey

Matamoros

GULF OF MEXICO

Havana

CUBA

Camagüey

DO
RE

San Luis Potosí

Tampico

Yucatán Channel

Santiago
de Cuba

HAITI

Isla de la
Juventad

Aguascalientes

Mérida

Cancún

Cayman
Islands (U.K)

Port-au-Prince

Guadalajara

León

Cape Corrientes

L. de Chapala

Bay of
Campeche

Yucatán
Peninsula

Kingston

JAMAICA

CARIB
S E

Manzanillo

Mexico City

Puebla

Orizaba

Veracruz

Campeche

Terminos
Lagoon

MEXICO

Balsas

Villahermosa

Belize City

Coatzacoalcos

Belmopan

Acapulco

Oaxaca

Gulf of
Tehuantepec

BELIZE

PACIFIC
OCEAN

GUATEMALA

Guatemala City

San Salvador

HONDURAS

Tegucigalpa

MEXICO

EL SALVADOR

NICARAGUA

Managua

Lake
Nicaragua

DOMINICAN
REPUBLIC

San José

Mosquitos
Gulf

PANAMA

COSTA
RICA

Panama
City

C O L O M B I A

Gulf of
Panama

GRENADA

ST VINCENT AND
GRENADINES

BARBADOS

ST KITTS AND
NEVIS

EL SALVADOR

COSTA RICA

TRINIDAD
AND TOBAGO

ST LUCIA

NICARAGUA

GUATEMALA

MEXICO,
CENTRAL AMERICA, & THE CARIBBEAN

Mexico stretches southward from the United States border, meeting the Pacific Ocean in the west and the Gulf of Mexico in the east. To the south are seven small nations—Guatemala, Belize, Honduras, El Salvador, Nicaragua, Costa Rica and Panama. To the east, tropical islands form a large arc around the Caribbean Sea.

Mexico forms a large triangle of land, with a tropical climate. A long thin peninsula, Baja California, runs parallel to the northeast coast. Another broader peninsula, Yucatán, sticks up like a thumb below the Gulf of Mexico. Mexico is a mountainous country, crossed by three branches of the Sierra Madre range. It is a land of deserts, tropical forests, and volcanoes, dotted with the spectacular ruins of ancient Native American civilizations, such as the Maya, Toltec, and Aztec. Mexico City,

built on the site of an ancient Aztec city, is a vast, polluted, sprawling centre of population. Earthquakes are common.

Today's Mexicans are descended from Native American peoples as well as from the Spanish who invaded and settled the region in the 1500s. Modern Mexico is an oil-producing country and attracts many tourists. It is a member of the North American Free Trade Agreement (NAFTA). However, many Mexicans remain very poor. Over the years many have headed north across the Rio Grande to seek illegal work in the USA.

To the south of Mexico, the mainland tapers to a thin strip of land called the Isthmus of Panama, which since 1914 has been crossed by the

Virgin Is.
J.K. & U.S.)
ANTIGUA & BARBUDA
ST. KITTS & NEVIS
Montserrat (U.K.)
Guadeloupe (FR.)
DOMINICA
Martinique (FR.)
ST. LUCIA
BARBADOS
ST. VINCENT & THE GRENADINES
GRENADA
TRINIDAD & TOBAGO

◄ *Color and craft*
This decorative craft work comes from the Jamaican tourist resort of Negril. It is probably inspired by the brilliantly colored fish of the Caribbean coral reefs.

Atlantic–Pacific shipping link of the Panama Canal. The seven small countries of Central America were also once ruled by Spain and they too have populations descended from Native American peoples as well as Spanish. They live mostly by farming tropical crops such as bananas, coffee, and sugarcane. The many poor people of the region have long been exploited by small numbers of the very rich and by brutal dictators. Central America has a long history of political strife and civil war.

The most widespread of the many languages spoken in Central America is Spanish. Most of the population is Roman Catholic. The whole region shares a love of music and dance, of poetry and political argument. Foods of the region have changed little since the days of the Aztecs, and include pancake-like tortillas, crisp tacos, beans, chili peppers, and avocados.

To the east, the Caribbean Sea is an arm of the Atlantic Ocean which is dotted with beautiful islands in warm, blue seas. They form two main island chains. The Greater Antilles include Cuba, Jamaica, Hispaniola (occupied by Haiti and the Dominican Republic), and Puerto Rico. The Lesser Antilles are more numerous, but smaller. They include the Virgin Islands, the Leeward and Windward Islands, Barbados and (along the South American coast) Trinidad and Tobago, Aruba, and the Netherlands Antilles.

Cuba is the largest Caribbean island, famous for its sugarcane, rum, and cigars. Since 1959 Cuba has had a communist government led by Fidel Castro. This has irritated Cuba's powerful neighbor to the north, the

◀ *Fancy ropework*
Based on traditional techniques, this Mexican showman demonstrates lassoing skills for an audience.

◀ *A tropical paradise*
The island of St. John is an unspoiled national park within the US Virgin Islands. It has a population of about 3,500.

United States, which forbids trade with the island. Florida, the nearest state, has become a haven for Cuban exiles.

The Caribbean region as a whole was once home to Native American peoples such as the Arawaks and the Caribs, after whom the region is named. Then came European invaders, explorers and pirates, including the Spanish, Dutch, French, and British. Most of today's Caribbean peoples are descended from West Africans who were brought in as slaves by the Europeans. Many small Caribbean islands became independent after the 1960s, but some remain dependencies of other countries.

Caribbean islanders live by fishing, farming, manufacture, and tourism. Favorite sports include baseball in Cuba and cricket in Jamaica and Barbados. The region is famous for its spectacular carnivals, which have encouraged a range of popular music styles, from calypso to salsa, from reggae to soca.

FACES OF ANCIENT MEXICO
This stone figure of a warrior is from the ancient Toltec capital of Tula, on the edge of Mexico's dry, northern regions. It is about 1,000 years old.
The ancient civilizations of "Mesoamerica" (Middle America) were among the greatest achievements of the Native American peoples who migrated southward through the continent tens of thousands of years ago.

▲ *Going to market, Guatemala*
The Maya people still live in Guatemala. Their women weave beautiful textiles, the patterns varying from one village to another.

Point. Gallinas

Barranquilla
Cartagena
Cristobal Colón

COLOMBIA

PANAMA

Cauca
Magdalena

VENEZUELA

Meta

Cape
Corrientes
Medellín
Pereira
Manizales
Ibagué **Bogotá**

COLOMBIA

Buenaventura
Cali
Neiva
Nevado del Huila
Guaviare

Pasto

Point
Galera

Quito

ECUADOR

Chimborazo

Caquetá

Putumayo

Guayaquil
Gulf of
Guayaquil

Iquitos

Amazon

Marañón

Point
Aguja
Piura
Chiclayo

BRAZIL

Ucayali

Trujillo
Nevado Huascarán
Chimbote

PERU

Callao
Huancayo
Lima

Cuzco
Guaporé

Paracas
Pen.
Nazca
Volcan
El Misti
Nevado
Ancohume
Mamoré

Arequipa
Lake
Titicaca
La Paz
BOLIVIA

PACIFIC
OCEAN
Cochabamba
Santa Cruz

Oruro
Lake
Poopó
Sucre

PERU

CHILE

ALTIPLANO

Potosi

Pilcomayo

PARAGUAY

ECUADOR

∇ **Mask of gold**
Rumors of gold treasur
brought Spanish invaders
the Andes in 1532. The
defeated and plundered t
great Inca empire.

BOLIVIA

THE NORTHERN ANDES

The Andes mountains extend down the whole length of South America, from north to south. They rise in Colombia, the country which borders the narrow land link with Central America, the Isthmus of Panama. The northern Andes continue to run parallel with the Pacific coast, through Ecuador, Peru and Bolivia.

▲ *A woman of the Bora*
The Bora are one of the indigenous peoples who live between the Caueta and Putumayo rivers in Colombia.

Colombia is a beautiful country, with coasts on both the Caribbean Sea and the Pacific Ocean. It takes in southwestern rain forests as well as dry, dusty lands and grassy plains. The mountains dominate the country, forming three main ranges. They are mined for gold, emeralds, salt, and coal. Coffee is grown in the foothills.

The chief cities of Colombia are either on the Caribbean coast, which is warm and humid, or in the cooler mountain regions. The latter include Medellín and the capital, Bogotá, which lies in the Cundinamarca basin, surrounded by peaks of the eastern range. The coca plant, used to make a dangerous drug called cocaine, is grown in parts of the countryside. The illegal trade in cocaine has created a problem of crime and gang warfare in the cities.

The Andes rise to 20,556 feet above sea level at Chimborazo in Ecuador. This country's name means "Equator" in Spanish, and the Pacific coast around the Equator is hot and moist. Bananas and sugarcane are grown here. In the cooler foothills of the Andes coffee is an important crop. The capital is Quito, sited on a plateau at 9,348 feet above sea level. To the east of the mountains are rain forests,

▲ *The biggest lake in South America*
Lake Titicaca is 12,497 feet above sea
level. Rushes which grow in the lake
are used to make houses and boats.

where oil is drilled.

Ecuador also governs the remote Galapagos Islands, which lie about 600 miles to the west, in the Pacific Ocean. The islands have a remarkable wildlife, which includes giant tortoises and marine iguanas (sea lizards).

In the 1400s, Peru was the center of the mighty Inca empire. This advanced Native American civilization produced beautiful textiles and jewellry in gold and precious stones. It was destroyed when the region was invaded by the Spanish in 1532. Ruined Inca cities such as Machu Picchu still perch high amongst the peaks of the Andes. Terraced hillsides allow crops such as potatoes to be grown in the mountains. The Peruvian Andes soar to 22,199 feet above sea level at Huascarán. Fishing is important along the foggy Pacific coast. In the far east, rivers flow through tropical forests into the Amazon.

Lake Titicaca lies high in the Andes, on the border with Bolivia. This inland country lies across the high plateau of the Altiplano and the

◄ *The sure-footed llama*
The llama is used for carrying goods in the Andes. This beast can pick its way along the narrowest of mountain paths.

humid eastern forests. The city of La Paz is the world's highest capital city, at 12,005 feet above sea level. Bolivia actually has twin capitals. La Paz is the seat of government, while Sucre, to the south, is the legal center of the nation. Bolivia produces tin, timber, rubber, and potatoes.

The lands of the northern Andes are home to many Native American peoples, such as the Quechua and Aymara, and their languages, crafts, customs, and music have all survived. The

▽ *Sounds of the Andes*
Native American traditions are kept alive in music. Popular instruments include the pan-pipes or rondador, drums, guitars, and flutes.

◄ *In Peru's misty mountains*
The Urumbaba river flows through steep gorges below the twin peaks of Machu Picchu and Huayna Picchu.

▼ *Baby pouch, Cuzco style*
This mother and baby belong to the Quechua, a people who live around the old Inca capital of Cuzco, in Peru.

whole region was ruled by Spain from the 1500s to the early 1800s, when revolutionaries such as the Venezuelan Simón Bolívar secured independence. Many people are of Spanish or mixed descent. Spanish is spoken throughout the region as well as a number of Native American languages. Most Northern Andeans are Roman Catholics, although the colorful festivals and pilgrimages of the region often show a clear link with Native American beliefs.

Although the region is rich in minerals and timber, many ordinary farmers and miners live in great poverty. This has led to political unrest and guerrilla warfare in many regions during the last 30 years.

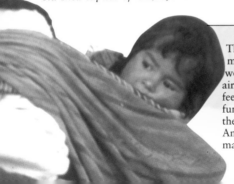

WILDLIFE OF THE ANDES
The most famous bird of the mountains is the Andean condor, the world's largest flying bird. It uses rising air currents to soar to heights of 13,000 feet on its huge wings. The shaggy-furred spectacled bear, which lives on the densely forested lower slopes of the Andes, takes its name from the markings around its eyes.

SOUTH AMERICA

VENEZUELA

GUYANA

SURINAME

▶ *Scarves and frills*
This Brazilian woman from the coastal city of Salvador de Bahía, on Brazil's Atlantic coast, wears the traditional costume of the region for a festival.

FRENCH GUIANA

Gulf of Venezuela
Netherlands Antilles
Maracaibo
Caracas
Port of Spain
TRINIDAD & TOBAGO
Lake Maracaibo
ANDES MTS.
Barcelona
Pico Bolívar
LLANOS
Orinoco
Orinoco Delta
VENEZUELA
Angel Falls
Georgetown
GUYANA
Paramaribo
G U I A N A   H I G H L A N D S
SURINAME
Cayenne
FRENCH GUIANA
Orinoco
COLOMBIA

Pico da Neblina
Negro
Branco
Macapá
Marajó Bay
Marajó I.
São Marcos Bay
Japurá
Belém
São Luis
Manaus
Amazon
Santarém
Tocantins
S E L V A S
Madeira
Teresina
Fortale
Juruá
Tapajós
Xingu
Purus
Jiparaná
Arinos
Araguaia
SE
Rio Branco
Aripuaná
Parnaíba
São F
PERU
SERRA DOS PARECIS
Guaporé
BRAZIL
BOLIVIA
Sobradinho Reservoir
Salvad
MATO GROSSO PLATEAU
Cuiabá
Brasília
Goiânia
B R A Z I L I A N
H I G H L A N D S

BRAZIL

Campo Grande
Uberlandia
Paraná
Belo Horizonte
Campos
PARAGUAY
São Paulo
Rio de Janeiro
Cape Frio
Itaipu Res.
Santos
Itguaçu Falls
Curitiba
SERRA DO MAR
ARGENTINA
Uruguay
Florianópolis
Santa Maria
Pôrto Alegre
URUGUAY
Patos Lagoon
Mirim Lake

BRAZIL
AND ITS NEIGHBORS

Brazil is South America's largest nation. It takes in the world's largest surviving area of rain forest, around the River Amazon. To the north, Venezuela lies on the River Orinoco, which flows into the Caribbean Sea. Three smaller countries also border the Caribbean coast—Guyana, Suriname, and French Guiana.

About a third of Brazil is taken up by tropical rain forests. These are crossed by hundreds of rivers, which drain into the wide, muddy waters of the Amazon, one of the world's two longest rivers. The river basin of the Amazon is the world's largest, covering 2,677,100 square miles. All kinds of rare plants, parrots, snakes and monkeys live in the dense, dripping rain forests, which are under threat from road builders, farmers, miners, and loggers.

Brazil is a vast country which also includes tropical grasslands, fertile plateaus and dry areas of scrub. Brazilian farmlands are the world's biggest suppliers of coffee and of soy beans, and the country is a major exporter of orange juice and sugar.

Most Brazilians live in the big cities of the Atlantic coast, such as Rio de Janeiro and São Paulo. The country has rich resources, but many of the population are poor people who live in shacks built on the city outskirts. Brasília, with its broad avenues and high-rise buildings, was specially built as a new capital in the 1960s. Portuguese is the chief language of Brazil. The land formed part of Portugal's overseas empire from 1500 until 1822. The original inhabitants included

▲ *Carnival in Rio*
For five days each year the Brazilian city of Rio de Janeiro is taken over by carnival dancers wearing spectacular costumes.

◀ *To the glory of God*
Nine out of ten Brazilians are Roman Catholics. This remarkable building is the Metropolitan Cathedral in Brasília, the modern capital.

a great variety of Native American peoples and cultures. Many of these were destroyed by European diseases, by persecution and murder. Scores of Brazil's surviving indigenous peoples, such as the Yanomami, face great problems today. Large numbers of Brazilians are of mixed descent, many of European origin (including Portuguese, Italian, and German), others of African origin.

tropical grassy plains of the Llanos. The beautiful Angel Falls (the highest in the world, with a drop of 3,211 feet) provide hydroelectric power, while Lake

The city of Rio de Janeiro has one of the world's most famous carnivals, which people celebrate to the rhythms of a dance called the samba. The national passion is undoubtedly soccer, and Brazil has one of the most successful national teams in the world.

To the northeast of Brazil, on the Caribbean coast, is Venezuela. This land, crossed by the Orinoco River, includes rain forests, high mountains, and the

▼ *Coffee for the world*
Coffee beans of the finest quality are grown in the Brazilian states of São Paolo, Paraná, Espírito Santo, and Minas Gerais.

Maracaibo, in the northwest, is rich in oil. Its capital is the northern city of Carácas. Venezuela was formerly ruled by Spain, and Spanish remains its chief language.

The three other countries on the Caribbean coast are Guyana, Suriname, and French Guiana. The first was once a British colony, the second was a Dutch colony and the third is still an overseas department of France. Most people live in the humid regions of the coast, while the

▶ **What a mouth!**
Razor-toothed piranha fish live in South America's muddy rivers. They are very fierce and can strip the flesh from a bone in seconds.

rain forests and mountains of the remote south are more sparsely populated. Crops include sugarcane, coffee, rice, and bananas. The Demerara river of Guyana has given its name to a famous type of brown sugar, while a type of hot red pepper is named for Cayenne, the capital of French Guiana. An important mineral resource of the region is bauxite, used in the making of aluminum. Kourou in French Guiana is a launch site for the Ariane rockets of the European Space Agency.

Many different ethnic groups live in these northern regions of the continent. They include Native American peoples, who like the Amazonian groups to the south, have had to struggle to survive. There are also Afro-Caribbeans, Asians and Europeans, all of whom have mingled over the years.

BENEATH THE SUGAR LOAF
Sugar Loaf Mountain towers above the port of Rio de Janeiro, topped by a statue of Jesus Christ with outstretched arms. Rio occupies a beautiful position on Guanabara Bay, but this sprawling city of nearly 10 million people includes large areas of slums and shanty towns. Rio was formerly the capital of Brazil.

> ▶ *The armour-plated mammals* There are 20 species of armadillo scattered through South America. Their skin is covered in horny plates. They hunt insects, snakes, and lizards.

Arica

ATACAMA DESERT

Iquique

BOLIVIA

Antofagasta

Calama

CHACO

Verde

Pilcomayo

Concepción

PARAGUAY

BRAZIL

Salta

GRAN

Bermejo

Asunción

Cuidad del Este

Ojos del Salado ▲

Copiapó

San Miguel de Tucumán

Formosa

Santiago del Estero

Resistencia

Corrientes

Posadas

Alto Paraná

Paraguay

Catamarca

SALADO

La Rioja

Parana

MESOPOTAMIA

Uruguay

Coquimbo
Pta. Lengua
de Vaca

Mar Chiquito

SIERRA DE CORDOBA

Córdoba

Concordia

Salto

Paysandú

San Juan

Santa Fe

Paraná

Negro

Aconcagua ▲

Mendoza

Rosario

Valparaiso

Santiago

San Luis

Río Cuarto

Buenos Aires

La
Plata

URUGUAY

Montevideo

Rancagua

San
Rafael

Salado

Río de La Plata
Pta. Norte
Cape San Antonio

Talca

PAMPAS

Chillán

Concepción
Pta. Lavapié

ARGENTINA

Bahía Blanca

Mar del Plata

Cape Corrientes

CHILE

Bahía Blanca

Temuco

Neuquén

Negro

Colorado

Valdivia
Pta. de la Galera

Limay

Viedma

San Matías Gulf

Osorno

Puerto Montt

Valdés Peninsula

Chiloé I.

Rawson

Chubut

C. Quilán

PATAGONIA

Chico

LOS CHONOS
ARCHIPELAGO

Comodoro Rivadavia

San Jorge Gulf

Lake Buenos
Aires

Deseado

C. Tres Puntas

Puerto Deseado

Peñas
Gulf

**PACIFIC
OCEAN**

Chico

Wellington I.

Santa Cruz

Puerto Santa Cruz

FALKLAND/MALVINAS
ISLANDS

Bahía
Grande

West
Falkland

Stanley

East
Falkland

REINA ADELAIDA
ARCHIPELAGO

Río Gallegos

Strait of Magellan

Punta Arenas

Tierra
del
Fuego

Santa Inés I.

Ushuaia

C. San Diego

Cape Horn

PARAGUAY

URUGUAY

ARGENTINA

CHILE

FALKLAND
ISLANDS

SOUTH GEORGIA (

ARGENTINA
AND ITS NEIGHBORS

The southern Andes mountains run down the border between Chile and Argentina to the cold and stormy waters of Tierra del Fuego and Cape Horn. This region includes some of the driest deserts in the world, bleak plateaus, sunny valleys, and rolling grasslands. Uruguay and Paraguay lie between Argentina and Brazil.

Argentina is the largest country in the southern part of South America. Its capital is Buenos Aires on the River Plate. More than eight out of every ten Argentineans are city dwellers. However it was the country's cattle-farming regions—the Pampa grasslands and the northeast—that in the last 150 years brought wealth to the country and attracted large numbers of settlers from Europe.

The Pampas were famed in the 1800s as the home of Argentina's wild cowboys, the Gauchos. Argentina's northern borders cross the tropical wilderness of the Gran Chaco, while its western borders follow the high peaks of the Andes range, which reach their highest point at Cerro Aconcagua (at 22,826 feet above sea level, the highest peak in all the Americas). In the shelter of the Andes, around the city of Mendoza, the climate is warm enough to grow fruit and grape vines. To the south are the windswept plateaus of Patagonia, largely given over to sheep farming. The port of Ushuaia is the southernmost town in the world.

Far out in the southern Atlantic Ocean are the windswept Falkland Islands, also grazed by large flocks of sheep. They are governed as a British colony but are claimed by Argentina, to whom they are the Islas Malvinas, and were at the centre of a bitter war between Britain and Argentina in 1982.

Northwards from Buenos Aires, across the River Plate, lies Montevideo, capital of Uruguay. This is another country which raises cattle and sheep, and whose rich grasslands and mild climate attracted European settlers. Neighboring Paraguay is far from any coast. Most of its people have chosen to farm the hills and plains of the east rather than settle in the inhospitable,

◀ Bottom of the world
Ushuaia, in Argentina,
is the world's most
southerly town, just
over 600 miles from
the North Pole. It has
long hours of sunlight
during the southern
summer, which
corresponds to winter
in the northern half of
the world.

hot region of the Gran Chaco.

To the west of the Andes is Chile, whose shape makes up the longest and narrowest country in this atlas. It includes one of the driest regions on Earth, the Atacama desert. However, it also includes fertile orchards and vineyards, the big capital city of Santiago and the specacular glaciers of the southern Andes. Chile also governs Easter Island, some 1,090 miles to the west in the south Pacific Ocean.

Southern South America includes many ancient Native American sites as well as colonial cities founded by Spanish invaders in the 1500s. During the days of rule by Spain many indigenous peoples were destroyed by savage wars or by diseases brought into the country by the Europeans. From the 1800s onward many immigrants

came to settle in the region as well as the Spanish. They included Italians, Basques, Germans, Central Europeans, Welsh, English, and Jewish people. Spanish is spoken throughout the region, alongside other European languages and some surviving Native American languages, such as those of the Guaraní and Mapuche.

Since the countries of the region broke away from Spanish rule in the nineteenth century,

▶ Chilean panorama
In Chile, the Andes mountain range
forms fantastic icy peaks, some of
which are active volcanoes.

they have known great political strife. Rule by military dictators has taken place in Argentina, Chile, Uruguay and Paraguay. In 1973 3,000 Chileans simply "disappeared"—tortured and murdered by the military when General Pinochet overthrew the elected government. A further 80,000 opponents of Pinochet were imprisoned. Three years later 10,000 Argentineans "disappeared" at the hands of death squads who supported military rule. Democracy returned to the region in the 1980s, but there are still serious economic problems and cities such as Santiago are ringed by slums and shanty towns.

Argentina and Chile are both countries which love literature, especially poetry. Folk songs and dance are a way of life, influenced both by Spanish and Native American traditions. A dance called the tango, first performed in the slums of Buenos Aires a hundred years ago, went on to become popular around the world. Popular sports include soccer, rugby, and automobile racing. The horse-riding skills of the Gauchos are reenacted in polo, strictly for the wealthy, and in a wild Argentinean sport called pato, which these days is a kind of basketball played on horseback.

The region inherited the Roman Catholic faith from its Spanish rulers, but there are also a growing number of Protestants, as well as Jews and people of other religions.

PLANT LIFE OF THE SOUTH
Southern South America includes a great variety of habitats, from coastal desert to savannah, from cloud forest to evergreen scrub. Plants of the region include all kinds of native species which have been exported to gardens and greenhouses around the world. These include cactuses, nasturtiums, monkey puzzle trees, fuchsias, and pampas grass.

TURKEY

SYRIA

IRAQ

IRAN

Istanbul
Gallipoli Bursa Sakarya Samsun *BLACK SEA*
                        PONTIC MOUNTAINS
Izmir Eskisehir **Ankara**
                  Tuz Lake Kizil ▲ Mt. Ararat
T U R K E Y Kayseri Lake Van Aras
Antalya Konya Gaziantep Diyarbakir Tabriz *C A S P I A N* TURKMENISTA
         TAURUS MTS. Adana   Lake Rasht *S E A*
Nicosia   Aleppo Euphrates Mosul Urmia ELBURZ ▲ Mt. Damavand
CYPRUS Tripoli **SYRIA** Horns Tigris As Sulaymaniyah MTS. Tehran Mashhad
Limassol **LEBANON**   Kirkuk Hamadan Qom *Dasht - e - Kavir*
Haifa Beirut **Damascus** *SYRIAN DESERT* Bakhtaran Kashan **I R A N**
ISRAEL Tel Aviv   **I R A Q** **Baghdad** ZAGROS MOUNTAINS Esfahan
Jerusalem **Amman**   Karbala   Yazd *Dasht - e - Lu*
JORDAN **JORDAN**   An Nasiriyah Ahvaz   Kerman
Elat Al Jawf Sakakah Basra Abadan Shiraz
EGYPT   **KUWAIT** Bushehr
         A N   N A F U D Kuwait   Bandar Abbas
                        Ad Damman Bandar e Lengeh
         Buraydah Ad Dahna **Al Manamah** Dubai Strait of Hormuz Jask
              Shqqra **BAHRAIN** **QATAR** **Abu Dhabi** Gulf of
Medina   Riyadh Doha **UNITED ARAB**
HIJAZ   **EMIRATES** ▲ Mu
S A U D I   A R A B I A   Jabal Ash Sham **O M A N**
Jiddah
Mecca   Masi
ASIR Tihamah *R u b ' a l   K h a l i*
         ▲ Jabal Sawda *(E m p t y   Q u a r t e r)*
RED SEA
Jaza'ir   Salalah
Farasan   Kuria Muria Is.
         Tarim
Al Hudaydah **San'a** **Y E M E N** Hadramaut
              Al Mukalla
Bab al Mandab Aden *Gulf of Aden* Socotra (YEMEN) **OMAN**
                                    'Abd al kuri

JORDAN

LEBANON

CYPRUS

SAUDI ARABIA

YEMEN

QATAR

BAHRAIN

UNITED ARAB
EMIRATES

KUWAIT

SOUTHWEST ASIA

This part of Asia includes the lands sometimes called the Near East or the Middle East. It stretches from the shores of the Black Sea southward to the Arabian peninsula.

Turkey is a large country whose most westerly part, around the beautiful old city of Istanbul, lies in Europe, across a strait called the Bosporus. Turkey has warm shores on the Mediterranean and Black Seas, but inland are grassy plains and mountain ranges which can be bitterly cold in winter. Its eastern neighbor, Iran, was formerly known as Persia. It includes fertile farmland and grasslands along the Caspian Sea, as well as bleak deserts and snowy mountain ranges. Turkey's southern neighbours are Syria and Iraq. They are part of a hot, very dry region. It is only made green by

▶ Followers of Islam This Muslim girl from San'a, the capital of Yemen, wears a black veil over her face.

the courses of two great rivers, the Tigris and Euphrates, which flow southwards into the Persian Gulf.

Southwest Asia's mild Mediterranean region includes the little island of Cyprus and the small nations of Lebanon and Israel, although these do border harsh desert terrain. The shores of the Dead Sea, a salt lake on the Israel-Jordan border, are 1,320 feet below sea level.

The great block of land known as the Arabian peninsula juts out into the Indian Ocean, with coasts on the Red Sea and the Persian Gulf. This is a region of trackless, shimmering deserts and rocky highlands, which have to be crossed by camel or four-wheel drive vehicles. It is dominated by the

▼ On the Gulf Dubai, an oil port on the Persian Gulf, is an ancient center of trade and fishing. Its nearby airport is an important stop off point on international routes.

▲ **Flare up in Iraq**
Natural gas is burned off at well-heads. Iraq's rich oil and gas reserves were one reason behind the Gulf War of 1991.

▶ **Tents in the desert**
Many desert peoples are nomads, following their herds from one seasonal pasture to another. This tent is in Rub' al Khali, Saudi Arabia's "Empty Quarter."

▼ **To the glory of God**
This breathtakingly beautiful mosque is in Isfahan, in Iran. It was begun in the year 1612, during the reign of Shah Abbas the Great.

Kingdom of Saudi Arabia, which is fringed by smaller Arab states, including Jordan, Yemen, Oman, the United Arab Emirates (UAE), Qatar, Bahrain and Kuwait.

Southwest Asia produces citrus fruits, dates, olives, nuts, cotton, and tobacco. It depends heavily on irrigation in its drier parts. The region's greatest resource by far is oil and natural gas, which has brought great wealth. However, these riches have not reached many of the region's poorer people, who live by herding camels and goats or fishing. Traditional crafts include the making of the world's finest carpets in Iran and Turkey.

Southwest Asia has an ancient and fascinating history. The world's first farmers raised animals and grew their crops around the Tigris and Euphrates about 10,000 years ago. Many great towns and cities grew up in the region, and it was also the birthplace of three world religions— Judaism, Christianity, and Islam. The city of Jerusalem is holy to all three faiths, while Mecca in Saudi Arabia is the holiest site of Islam and a center of pilgrimage.

Southwest Asian peoples include Greeks, Turks, Jews, and Iranians. The homeland of the Kurdish people is divided between Turkey, Iraq, and Iran. Arabs live in much of the region, forming a number of different cultural groups and nationalities, from the Palestinians in the state of Israel to the Marsh Arabs who live in the wetlands of southern Iraq.

The Middle East has always been at a crossroads of cultures, with trading routes stretching

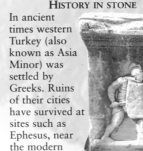

HISTORY IN STONE

In ancient times western Turkey (also known as Asia Minor) was settled by Greeks. Ruins of their cities have survived at sites such as Ephesus, near the modern Turkish settlement of Selçuk, to the south of Izmir.

eastward to Central Asia and China, westward to Europe and North Africa, southward to India and East Africa. Tragically it has also been devastated by wars for much of its history. Recent years have seen war and strife through most of the region, from Cyprus to Israel and Lebanon, to Iraq, Kuwait, and Iran.

◀ *A holy city Qom, in Iran, is sacred to Muslims of the Shia sect. Religion has played an important part in the government of Iran since the king, or Shah, was overthrown in 1979.*

81

AFGHANISTAN

NEPAL

BHUTAN

BANGLADESH

PAKISTAN

INDIA

SRI LANKA

MALDIVES

TURKMENISTAN

TAJIKISTAN

Mazar-e-Sharif

Herat

HINDU

AFGHANISTAN   Kabul   DISPUTED

Farah   Khyber Pass   Peshawar   AREA   K2

Islamabad   Srinagar   KARAKORAM

Qandahar   Rawalpindi   JAMMU &
RIGESTAN   KASHMIR
DESERT   Faisalabad Lahore

Quetta   Amritsar

PAKISTAN   Multan   PUNJAB   Tibet (CHINA)

BALUCHISTAN   Sukkur Bahawalpur   Nanda Devi   NEPAL

PLATEAU   Hyderabad   GREAT INDIAN DESERT   Delhi   Annapurna   Mt Everest   Thimphu

Karachi   (THAR DESERT)   New Delhi Bareilly   Katmandu   BHUTAN

Gulf of Kachch   Jodhpur   Jaipur Agra   Lucknow   Ghagara   Brahmaputra

Ajmer   Yamuna   Kanpur   Gauhati

Udaipur   Kota Gwalior   Allahabad   Varanasi   Patna   NAGA

Jamnagar   Ahmadabad Indore Bhopal   Ganges

Bhavnagar   Vadodara   Narmada   Jabalpur   BANGLADESH Imphal

Surat   I N D I A   Jamshedpur   Asanol   Dhaka   MYANMAR

Aurangabad   Nagpur   Raipur   Calcutta   Khulna   Chittagong   (BURMA)

Mumbai   DECCAN   Cuttack   Mouths of the Ganges

(Bombay)   Pune   Mahanadi

Solapur   Godavari

Kolhapur   Hyderabad

Hubli-Dharwar   Krishna   Vishakhapatnam

Kurnool   Vijayawada

Penner   Nellore

Mangalore   Bangalore

Mysore   Chennai
                (Madras)
Kozhikode   Coimbatore

Cochin   Tiruchchirappalli

Madurai   Palk Strait

Trivandrum   Jaffna   Andaman
                Trincomalee   &
C. Comorin   Nicobar
Gulf of Mannar   SRI LANKA   (India)

MALDIVES   Colombo   Kandy

INDIAN   Pidurutalagala
OCEAN   Galle

82

INDIA AND ITS NEIGHBORS

Southern Asia forms a massive triangle of land which is bordered by the Indian Ocean. It is called the Indian subcontinent. Where it meets the countries to the north, the land has been squeezed up and crumpled, to form the world's highest mountain ranges.

The Karakoram and Himalaya ranges run in a great arc from northern Afghanistan, through northern Pakistan and India to the small mountain kingdoms of Nepal and Bhutan. The peaks soar to 29,021 feet above sea level at Mount Everest or Qomolangma, on the border between Nepal and Tibet (a region governed by China). This is the highest mountain in the world.

Many streams and rivers rise in these snow-capped mountains. The mighty Indus River flows into the Arabian Sea, fed by the Jhelum, Chenab, Ravi, and Sutlej waterways which cross Pakistan's Punjab region. The River Ganges flows southeast, crossing the fertile plains of northern India before joining the Brahmaputra in Bangladesh. The Irawaddy, another long river, crosses the country of Myanmar

▼ Street performers
A deadly cobra sways to the music of a snake charmer. India's big cities bustle with busy crowds, street vendors, beggars, and showmen.

(or Burma) to the east. India is a very large country which includes the forested hills of the Eastern and Western Ghats, sandy deserts, the plateau country of the Deccan, and teeming, colorful cities such as Delhi, Bombay, and Calcutta. The climate is extremely hot for much of the year, relieved when the monsoon winds bring heavy downpours of rain. Indian Ocean islands include beautiful, tropical Sri Lanka and a long chain of coral reefs and islands, the Maldives. The

▶ *The Taj Mahal, near Agra*
The domes of this great marble tomb are reflected in pools of water. It was completed in 1653.

latter are so low-lying that they could disappear beneath the waves if the world's climate were to become warmer, causing a rise in sea levels.

Crops grown by the farmers of the subcontinent include jute, tea, coconuts, sugarcane, cotton, millet, sorghum, and corn. Drought is common in many regions, while coastal regions of Bangladesh often experience severe flooding. Most of the region is rural, but the great cities of India and Pakistan include factories and workshops producing textiles of cotton and silk, heavy machinery, iron, and steel. India manufactures computer equipment. Bombay produces films and videos.

The population of India numbers 969,700,000. Pakistan numbers about 137,800,000 and Bangladesh 122,200,000. It is hard to feed so many mouths and poverty is widespread. The mountainous nations to the north and the Maldive islands are thinly populated.

This part of Asia is home to very many different peoples and ancient cultures. About 845 different languages may be heard in India alone. Many religions have also grown up in this region over the

AT THE MARKET
Brilliantly colored dyes and powders are laid out at a market in the southern Indian city of Mysore. India's street markets offer bright bales of cotton and silk, silver jewelry, carved wooden boxes and trays, statues of Hindu gods, wreaths of flowers, and sweet sticks of incense. There are also all kinds of practical goods for sale, such as radios, batteries, pots, and pans. Tailors make up shirts, trousers, or fine saris. Stalls sell sweet, milky tea as well as delicious snacks.

▶ *The biggest of the cats*
The powerful but increasingly rare Bengal tiger lives in the forests of Nepal, India and Bangladesh. It is protected in special reserves.

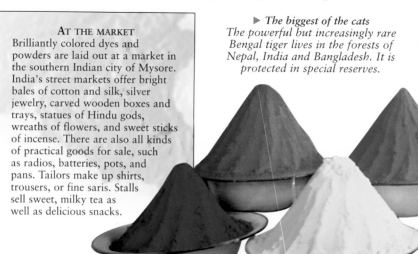

▶ **The Buddhist temples of Myanmar**
In ancient times Pagan, the City of a Thousand Temples, was the capital of Burma, or Myanmar. Most Burmese still worship at Buddhist temples today.

ages, including Hinduism, Buddhism, Sikhism and Jainism. Afghanistan, the Maldives, Pakistan and Bangladesh are all Muslim nations, and many Muslims also live in India. All these faiths have inspired a wealth of religious ceremonies, dances, and festivals.

The Indian subcontinent has seen many splendid civilizations come and go, from that of Mohenjo-Daro (dating back about 4,500 years) to that of the Moguls who ruled India from 1526 until the 1800s. India, Pakistan, Bangladesh, Myanmar, and Sri Lanka all went on to become part of the British empire, but have been independent nations since 1947-1948.

India today is the world's largest democracy. Pakistan and Myanmar have known long periods of military

▲ **The holy Ganges**
Hindu pilgrims come to the holy city of Varanasi, in northern India. They bathe in the sacred waters of the River Ganges.

rule while Afghanistan has suffered civil war and many violent changes of government. Many peoples from the Indian subcontinent have, over the ages, settled in other parts of the world. There are Indian, Pakistani or Bangladeshi communities in Southeast Asia, East and South Africa, Great Britain, Canada, Australia, the Caribbean, and the Pacific.

85

► **On the South China Sea** Traditional wooden sailing ships may still be seen. They are called junks.

NORTH KOREA

SOUTH KOREA

MONGOLIA

RUSSIA

Hovsgol Lake

KAZAKHSTAN

Ulaangom

Darhan

Edernet

Choybalsan Tamsagbulag

HENTYN MTS.

Qiqihar

Harbin

Mudanjiang

Ulan Bator

HANGAYN MTS.

MONGOLIA

ALTAI MTS.

Fuhai

Hovd

Changchun

Jilin

Ch'ŏngjin

Fushun

Shenyang

Anshan

NORTH KOREA

Hamhung

Ebinur Hu

Karamay

Chifeng

Jinzhou

P'yongyang

Wonsan

Yining

Kuytun

Dzungaria

Dalardzadgad

GOBI DESERT

Baotou

Beijing

Tangshan

Dalian

Korea Bay

Kaesong

Seoul

SOUTH KOREA

Ürümqi

Hami

Shizuishan

Tianjin

Bo Gulf

Weihai

Pu...

TIAN SHAN

Aksu

Bosten Lake

Turfan Depression

MU US DESERT

Shijiazhuang

Yantai

YELLOW SEA

Zibo

Qingdao

KYRGYZSTAN

TAKLIMAKAN DESERT

Yumen

Yinchuan

Taiyuan

Jinan

Kashi

ALTUN SHAN

QILIAN SHAN

Xining

Lanzhou

Huang He

Xuzhou

Hongze Lake

Nantong

Cheju I.

EAST CHINA SEA

Mt. K2

Hotan

Qinghai Lake

Huang He

Zhengzhou

Nanjing

Shanghai

KARAKORAM

KUNLUN SHAN

Xi'an

Macheng

Chao Lake

Hangzhou

Ningbo

INDIA

PLATEAU OF TIBET

BAYAN HAR SHAN

C H I N A

Yichang

Wuhan

Poyang Lake

Linhai

Siling Lake

TANGGULA SHAN

SICHUAN BASIN

Chang Jiang

Dongting Lake

Nanchang

Wenzhou

Tangra Lake

Nam Lake

Qamdo

Chengdu

Chongqing

Changsha

Fuzhou

Mt. Everest

Lhasa

Leshan

Luzhou

NEPAL

Xigaze

BHUTAN

Salween

DALOU SHAN

Hengyang

Zhangzhou

Xiamen

Taipei

TAIWAN

Kaohsiung

Guiyang

NAN LING MTS.

Shantou

MYANMAR (Burma)

Mekong

AILAO MTS.

Xiaguan

Kunming

Liuzhou

Xi Jiang

Guangzhou

Hong Kong

MACAO

LAOS

VIETNAM

Gejiu

Nanning

Pingxiang

Zhanjiang

Gulf of Tongkin

Haikou

Hainan

GREATER HINGGAN

LESSER HINGGAN

Amur

Tonghua

Taiwan Strait

CHINA

HONG KONG

TAIWAN

► **Pagoda roofs**
Pagodas are graceful towers with many storeys. The pagoda design came into China from India, along with the Buddhist faith, over 1,500 years ago.

CHINA AND ITS NEIGHBORS

The People's Republic of China is the world's third biggest nation, occupying an area about the size of western Europe. For the last 50 years the southern Chinese island of Taiwan has had its own government. To the north is Mongolia, and in the northeast are North and South Korea.

China is the giant of the Far East, with a population of 1,236,700,000—the largest in the world. Most Chinese live in the eastern half of the country. This is crossed to the north by the Huang He or Yellow River, which takes its name from the thick mud which colors its waters. The river winds through a rich soil called loess, which has been blown here from deserts to the north. Northern China has bitterly cold winters and warm summers. It produces wheat and fruit, and is rich in resources such as coal and timber.

Many large cities are in the north, including the capital, Beijing. Beijing is growing rapidly into a modern city of high-rise buildings and highways. However it still contains many ancient buildings, such as the Imperial Palace, known as the Forbidden City, and the Temple of Heaven, or Tiantan.

Central China is crossed by the world's third longest river, the Chang Jiang (sometimes called the Yangze). It runs from the western mountains through the province of Sechuan. After passing through steep gorges and a series of dams, it spills across the fertile plains of the east. The great port of Shanghai, by the East China Sea, lies on a tributary of the Chang Jiang.

Southern China includes the island of Hainan, sunny Yunnan province, misty lakes and rivers, the great cities of Guangzhou and Hong Kong. The latter, a center of international business, was a British colony until 1997.

◀ **Water and sky**
*Aberdeen, on the southern side of
Hong Kong's Victoria Island, takes in
both towering skyscrapers and
sampans, small boats used as floating
homes.*

Standard Chinese is spoken by
more people than any other
language in the world, and the
southern dialect of Cantonese is
also widely spoken.

Southern China's warm, humid
climate is ideal for growing rice,
which is China's staple crop. The
coast of the South China Sea is
sometimes battered by seasonal
tropical storms called typhoons.

China is ringed by high
mountains and fierce deserts. The
remote west includes areas such
as Xinjiang and Tibet, which at
times in its history has been an
independent country. Nine out of
ten Chinese belong to the Han
people, but there are over 50
other "minority" peoples,
distinguished by their own
customs, languages, or religions.

The Chinese have been
influenced by various
beliefs. Confucianism is a
belief in social order
and respect for one's
ancestors. Daoism is
based upon a belief
in harmony and
nature. Buddhism
first came to China
from India. The
three beliefs
became mingled
over the ages.

Chinese
civilization grew up
over 5,000 years ago.
China became a united
empire in 221BC, and
rule by emperors
continued until 1911. The
Chinese were great poets,
artists and technical innovators.
They invented paper, printing,
gunpowder, and the manufacture
of silk. They produced the
world's finest pottery, known as
porcelain—or "china."

In the 1930s and 40s China
saw invasion by the Japanese and
a bitter civil war between
Communists and Nationalists.
The Japanese were defeated and
the Communists came to power

▲ **Planting rice, South Korea**
*Women plant out rice seedlings in paddies
fields near Andong, in central South
Korea. Rice is the staple diet of the Far
East.*

CHINA AND ITS NEIGHBORS

FAR EASTERN FOODS
Chinese cooking is said to be among the best in the world. It varies greatly from one region to another. Favorite dishes include rice, noodles and dumplings, duck and pork, fish, fresh green vegetables and soy bean curd. Some regions like hot and peppery tastes, with chilis and peanuts.

◄ *Getting around*
Tram, taxi, rail or ferry are all travel options in Hong Kong, the former British colony which returned to Chinese rule in 1997.

in 1949. The Nationalists fled to the island of Taiwan, where they set up a rival government. Taiwan today is an international center of business and manufacture. Mainland China is still ruled by the Communist Party, but it now promotes big business rather than following Communist policies.

For hundreds of years Chinese people have settled overseas and brought their culture to other parts of the world. There are large Chinese communities in Southeast Asia, North America, and Western Europe. Dragon dancers may be seen celebrating Chinese New Year on the streets of San Francisco, London, or Singapore.

The homeland of the Mongol

peoples is divided between China, the Russian Federation and the independent republic of Mongolia. This is a large but sparsely populated country, with empty, rolling grasslands and desert. Many of its people are nomads, living by herding sheep and camels. Some still live in round tents called gers or yurts. In the Middle Ages Mongol horsemen conquered China to the south and also invaded large areas of Central Asia and Eastern Europe.

The Korean peninsula is the centre of another ancient civilization. In 1950-1953 the country was torn apart by a bitter war between the communist world and the west. Korea became two separate, hostile countries. North Korea remained communist, while South Korea became a major center of business and manufacture.

▼ *The Great Wall of China*
This wall defended the ancient Chinese empire against northern invaders. Thousands of miles of the wall may still be seen today.

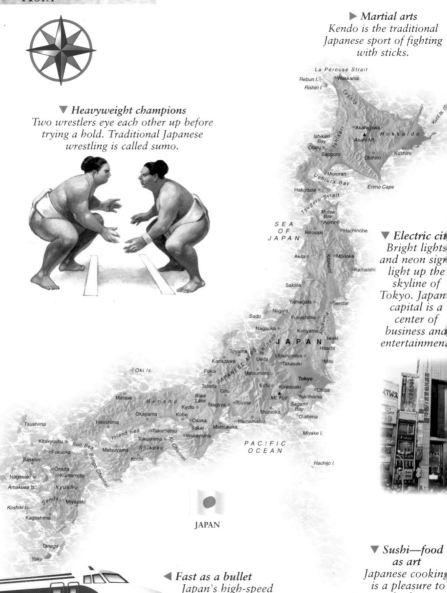

▶ **Martial arts**
Kendo is the traditional
Japanese sport of fighting
with sticks.

▼ **Heavyweight champions**
Two wrestlers eye each other up before
trying a hold. Traditional Japanese
wrestling is called sumo.

▼ **Electric cit**
Bright lights
and neon sig
light up the
skyline of
Tokyo. Japan
capital is a
center of
business and
entertainmen

JAPAN

◀ **Fast as a bullet**
Japan's high-speed
Bullet Train is one
of the most
famous
locomotives
in the
world.

▼ **Sushi—food
as art**
Japanese cookin
is a pleasure to
look at as
well as t
eat.

90

JAPAN

A long string of more than 3,000 islands makes up the country of Japan. The islands lie off the eastern coast of Asia, between the Sea of Japan and the open waters of the Pacific Ocean. The four largest ones are called Kyushu, Shikoku, Honshu, and Hokkaido.

Lying on the rim of the Pacific Ocean, Japan lies in one of the world's danger zones for earthquakes and volcanic eruptions. Inland, the islands are mostly forested and mountainous, so most of the agricultural regions, as well as the cities, are to be found on the flat lands around the coast.

Japan is famous for its spring blossoms, and much of the country has a mild climate. However, northern winters can be cold and very snowy, while southern islands extend toward the warmth of the tropics.

Japan grows rice, fruit, vegetables, and tea. It has a big fishing fleet and there is a huge market for the catch. Japan has few natural resources but has become one of the world's leading industrial countries, selling cars and electrical goods around the world. The capital city, Tokyo, is on the island of Honshu. Its buildings have spread out to merge with those of Yokohama, forming one of the largest town areas of the world. Over three quarters of all Japanese are city dwellers.

Japan is famous for its ancient buildings as well as for its modern banks and offices. They include temples and shrines of the Buddhist and Shinto religions, as well as tall castles. Japan's history was made by emperors with splendid courts, by armored knights called samurai and by great artists and architects. Its craft workers were masters of design, producing beautiful pottery. During the World War II, between 1940 and 1945, Japan invaded a large area of the Far East and fought against the Allies. In 1945 terrible atomic bombs dropped on the cities of Hiroshima and Nagasaki brought this war to an end.

Nearly all the people of Japan are Japanese, although a small number in the north are descended from the islands' first inhabitants, a people called the Ainu. Japan still has an emperor, but today real power lies with its democratic parliament.

MYANMAR
(BURMA)

LAOS

THAILAND

CAMBODIA

PHILIPPINES

BRUNEI

VIETNAM

SINGAPORE

MALAYSIA

INDONESIA

SOUTHEAST ASIA

The tropical lands of southeast Asia lie between the Indian and Pacific Oceans. The mainland tapers into a long, thin peninsula, which breaks up into a chain of volcanic islands. Thailand, Laos, Cambodia, and Vietnam occupy the north of the region. Malaysia, Singapore, Brunei and Indonesia occupy the south, while the Philippines lie in the east.

◀ *Whatever the weather*
Broad-brimmed, cone-shaped straw hats are worn by field workers in many parts of Southeast Asia. They keep off both the hot sun and the monsoon rains.

Southeast Asia is home to a fascinating mixture of hundreds of different peoples. There are the Thais, the Hmong, Khmer, Cham, Lao, Annamese, Chinese, Indians, Dayaks, Iban, Toradja, Moluccans, Filipinos, all with their own languages and cultures. Religions include Buddhism, Hinduism, Islam, and Christianity. Many Southeast Asians have settled overseas, in the Netherlands, Australia, and North America. Thai and Malaysian cooking has become popular around the world.

Much of the southeast Asian mainland is occupied by Thailand. This country, once known as Siam, descends from the mountains along the border with Myanmar (Burma) to the network of rivers which flow into the Gulf of Thailand. A thin sliver of territory stretches southward down the Isthmus of Kra to the Malaysian border. The land is green with teak forests and rice paddies. Tourists visit Thailand to see its beautiful beaches and its ancient Buddhist temples. Thailand is a kingdom and was the only nation in the region to avoid foreign rule in the 1800s and 1900s.

The three countries to the east, Cambodia, Laos, and Vietnam, all came under French rule at that time and were known as Indo-China. They too have tropical forests, highland regions, and flooded rice paddies. They are linked by the Mekong, a great river that flows from China right across the region into southern Vietnam. These are beautiful countries with ancient cultures and splendid Buddhist temples.

Sadly, they have all seen terrible fighting in the last 60 years. This included

◀ Green terraces, Thailand
Rice has been grown on the terraced hillsides of Southeast Asia for thousands of years. They are flooded by irrigation channels.

countries in the region the forests have been devastated by logging over the years, and by fires which have caused widespread air pollution. The Malaysian capital, Kuala Lumpur, is a center of international business, which boasts the world's highest office buildings, the twin 1,482 foot-high Petronas Towers.

Another world business center is Singapore, built on islands across the Johor Strait. Singapore was ruled

Japanese invasion in the 1940s, a French bid to take the region back under its rule in the 1950s, the terrible Vietnam War of the 1960s and 70s, in which the United States failed to defeat the Vietnamese Communists, and a brutal civil war in Cambodia in the 1970s and 80s. Today these nations are looking forward to more peaceful times.

Malaysia takes up the southern part of the long Southeast Asian peninsula, but also includes the regions of Sarawak and Sabah on the island of Borneo. The country produces rice, rubber, and oil. Its rain forests are home to lush plants and strange animals such as the orangutan, a giant ape. Like other

▶ Peace of the spirit
Thailand is a Buddhist country and has many sacred sites and statues. There are more than 27,000 Buddhist temples.

▶ A floating market
Vegetables and fruit are traded directly from small boats on this waterway near Bangkok.

▼ City by the sea
Singapore is a great center of trade. Its population of nearly 3 million includes people of Chinese, Malay, Tamil, and European descent.

by Britain from 1858 until 1959. Much of the state's territory is now taken up by the modern buildings of Singapore City, where nearly all the population lives. In the 1960s Singapore was briefly united with Malaysia, but it broke away to become an independent state.

The rapid growth of economic development in countries such as Singapore and Malaysia in the 1980s gave them the nickname of "Asian tigers." However, by the end of the 1990s all Far Eastern economies seemed to face a less certain future.

The Sultanate of Brunei is a small independent nation on the north coast of Borneo. Oil wealth has made its ruler the richest man in the world. Much of the country is covered in tropical forest, which is being damaged by illegal logging. Plantations produce bananas and rubber.

Indonesia, formerly ruled by the Dutch, is a nation of islands—many thousands of them. The largest are Sumatra, Java, southern Borneo, Sulawesi, and western New Guinea, which is called Irian Jaya. The forested islands lie on the Pacific rim, notorious for it violent volcanoes. The destruction of the island of Krakatoa in 1883 was the worst eruption in the world's recorded history. The Indonesian population today numbers more than 204 million, and is the

world's largest Islamic nation. Its government is under increasing pressure to improve its record on human rights and democracy, especially on the island of East Timor, which it occupied in 1975, and in Irian Jaya. The islands produce rice, rubber, coffee, oil, and natural gas. The beautiful island of Bali, with its unique form of Hinduism, attracts tourists from all over the world. Indonesia is famous for its patterned textiles, dyed by methods known known as batik and ikat.

Finally we travel eastward to the Philippines, on the edge of the open Pacific Ocean. This maze of 7,000 small islands was once ruled by Spain and later by the United States. It became independent in 1946. The Philippines produce rice, timber, electrical goods, and garments. Its people are mostly Roman Catholic.

DRAGONS AND BUTTERFLIES

The volcanic islands and tropical rain forests of Southeast Asia support many weird and wonderful animals. Many are rare or threatened by the destruction of the forests where they live. The komodo dragon of Indonesia is the world's biggest lizard. The smallest mammal lives in Thailand—a bat that is the size of a bumblebee. There are other spectacular species like giant butterflies, sea snakes, and flying frogs.

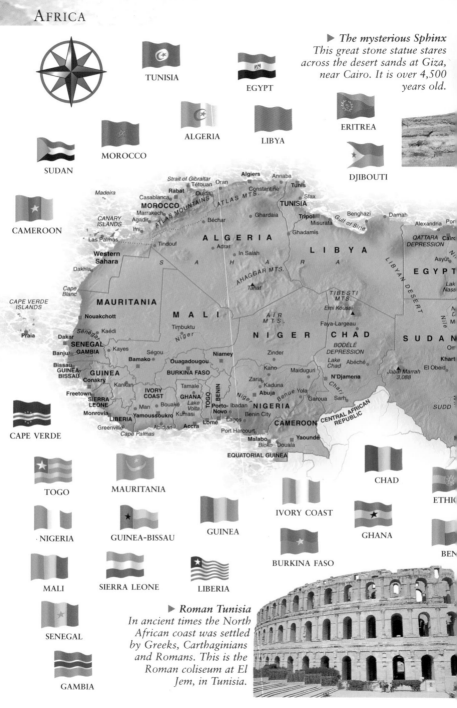

► The mysterious Sphinx
This great stone statue stares across the desert sands at Giza, near Cairo. It is over 4,500 years old.

TUNISIA

EGYPT

ALGERIA

LIBYA

ERITREA

MOROCCO

SUDAN

DJIBOUTI

CAMEROON

CAPE VERDE

TOGO

MAURITANIA

CHAD

NIGERIA

GUINEA-BISSAU

GUINEA

IVORY COAST

GHANA

ETHIO

BURKINA FASO

BEN

MALI

SIERRA LEONE

LIBERIA

SENEGAL

► Roman Tunisia
In ancient times the North African coast was settled by Greeks, Carthaginians and Romans. This is the Roman coliseum at El Jem, in Tunisia.

GAMBIA

NORTH AND WEST AFRICA

The Sahara is the world's biggest desert. This wilderness of sand, gravel and rock swelters under a burning sun. To the north it is fringed by the green lands of the Mediterranean. To the south it gives way to dusty grasslands, the humid Guinea coast, the swamps of southern Sudan, and the mountains of Ethiopia.

The countries of Morocco, Algeria and Tunisia are sometimes known as the Maghreb, the "far west" of the Arab world. They are also home to the Berber peoples. Their coastal lands enjoy a mild climate, and are farmed for wheat, olives, oranges, and vegetables. Southwards the land rises to the ranges of the Atlas mountains, whose valleys are grazed by goats and sheep.

In the south of these countries are the shifting sands of the Sahara, crossed by ancient trading routes. Peoples such as the Tuareg cross the desert's ancient trading routes by camel. They camp at oases, where water supplies make it possible to grow dates and figs. The state of Western Sahara, rich in phosphates, is claimed by

▶ *Arabic styles*
A modern wall decoration in Tunisia echoes traditional styles of Arab architecture. The Arabs invaded North Africa nearly 1,400 years ago.

Morocco.

Africa's northeastern countries, Libya and Egypt, are also Arab lands. Their deserts are scorched dry, but in the east they are crossed by the Nile, the world's longest river. Its banks provide a narrow, fertile strip and a green delta region on the Mediterranean coast. Africa's first great civilization grew up along the Nile more than 5,000 years ago. Egypt's capital, Cairo, is the biggest city in Africa. Cotton and textiles are important exports.

Branches of the Nile also cross through the lands to the

◀ **Bridge over the Nile**
Cairo, the capital of Egypt, lies on the River Nile. Egypt has always depended on this great waterway for its survival.

south of Egypt. Sudan is Africa's largest country, with deserts in the north, green mountains in the west and a vast wetland region called the Sudd in the south. While the north of the country lies within the Arab world, the south is home to a wide variety of Black African farming and cattle herding peoples, such as the Dinka and Shilluk. Ethiopia is a mountainous land which becomes desert in the east. It grows grain crops such as corn, sorghum, and teff, as well as coffee and sugarcane. Two small countries, Eritrea and Djibouti, share its Red Sea coastline.

The lands to the south of the Sahara are known as the Sahel countries. They include Mauritania, Mali, Burkina Faso, Niger, and Chad. Desert sands are blown southward by seasonal winds into the Sahel's dry grasslands, which are grazed by cattle and goats. This whole belt of Africa suffers greatly from drought and famine is common. The people are often desperately poor.

Farther south, the climate becomes more moist and the soil richer. West Africa is a great bulge of land ranged around the Gulf of Guinea, crossed by branches

A camel's eye view
The spectacular pyramids of Giza mark royal tombs, dating back to the early days of ancient Egypt. Camels were not introduced into Egypt until much later.

of the River Burkina or Volta, and by the mighty River Niger. It includes plateaus and rolling hill country, descending to tropical forest and swamps along the humid, palm-fringed coast. The region has rich natural resources, such as oil and diamonds, but most of the people have remained poor. Crops include cocoa, rubber, palm-oil, peanuts, and cotton.

The countries of the west are the Cape Verde Islands, Senegal and Gambia, Guinea and Guinea-Bissau, Sierra Leone, and Liberia. The central gulf states are Côte d'Ivoire, Ghana, Togo, Benin and Nigeria, whose population of over 107 million is the biggest in Africa.

▲ **Ethiopian bread**
Injera is a flat, doughy bread which is eaten in Ethiopia. It is used to mop up meat and vegetable stews.

DESERT SURVIVORS
The Sahara is one of the most inhospitable regions on Earth, but many creatures have learned how to survive in the desert. They include deadly scorpions (right), a type of antelope called the addax and the fennec, a fox whose big ears help it to lose heat. The sandgrouse flies to oases where it traps drops of water in its feathers.

The eastern gulf states, around the Bight of Biafra, take in Cameroon, Equatorial Guinea and the offshore islands of São Tomé and Príncipe.

Islam is the religion of the Saharan countries, but the southern regions of West Africa and southern Sudan are Christian. The Ethiopian Church is over 1,600 years old. In many areas, traditional African beliefs in spirits are still popular.

Hundreds of different peoples live in the Sahel and West African countries, including the Malinke, Ewe, Kabre, Kulani, Kanuri, Ibo, and Yoruba. In ancient times there were powerful empires in both Ethiopia and West Africa. Ethiopia did remain independent, but most of the region suffered raids by slave traders, foreign invasion, and colonial rule. Colonial languages including English, French, and Portuguese may still be heard. All the countries of the region are now independent.

AFRICA

Fishing in Lake Malawi
Fishermen set up a ring of nets. This lake, 3,579 miles long, is a drowned section of the Great Rift Valley.

ANGOLA

BOTSWANA

RWANDA

SOMALIA

ZIMBABWE

BURUNDI

ZAMBIA

MOZAMBIQUE

SEYCHELLES

CENTRAL AFRICAN REPUBLIC

MALAWI

CONGO

UGANDA

KENYA

GABON

SOMALIA

CENTRAL AFRICAN REPUBLIC

Berbera

Cape Caseyr

CHAD

Bozoum

Bangassou

Bomu

SUDAN

ETHIOPIA

Juba

Bangui

CAMEROON

Congo

Uele

UGANDA

Lake Turkana

KENYA

Mogadishu

SÃO TOMÉ & PRÍNCIPE

Libreville

REP. OF CONGO

Mbandaka

Kisangani

Margherita Peak

Kampala

Mt. Kenya

Cape Lopez

GABON

DEMOCRATIC REP. OF CONGO

RWANDA

Lake Victoria

Mwanza

Nairobi

Kismayu

INDIAN OCEAN

Brazzaville

Kinshasa

Kigali

Bukavu

Bujumbura

BURUNDI

Kilimanjaro

Mombasa

SEYCHELLES

Cabinda (ANGOLA)

Matadi

Kananga

Kasai

Sankuru

Dodoma

Zanzibar

Dar-es-Salaam

MAURITIUS

Luanda

ANGOLA PLATEAU

Lake Tanganyika

Rufiji

TANZANIA

Aldabra Is.

Likasi

Lake Mweru

Lake Nyasa

C. Delgado

COMOROS

C. d'Ambre

Lobito

Huambo

Lubumbashi

Ndola

MALAWI

Antisiranana

A N G O L A

Namibe

Cunene

Cubango

Cuito

ZAMBIA

Lusaka

Lilongwe

Moçambique

Mahajanga

Etosha Pan

Okavango Delta

Livingstone

Zambezi

Harare

Blantyre

MOZAMBIQUE

Toamasina

NAMIBIA

Windhoek

BOTSWANA

ZIMBABWE

Bulawayo

Beira

Antananarivo

MADAGASCAR

MAURITIUS

KALAHARI DESERT

Gaborone

Limpopo

Fianarantsoa

Réunion (France)

NAMIB DESERT

Pretoria

Maputo

Johannesburg

Mbabane

SWAZILAND

C. Ste. Marie

NAMIBIA

KAROO

Great Karoo

Kimberley

Maseru

Durban

SOUTH AFRICA

High Veld

LESOTHO

DRAKENSBERG

SOUTH AFRICA

Orange

Cape of Good Hope

Cape Town

Cape Agulhas

East London

Port Elizabeth

MADAGASCAR

LESOTHO

Traditional lives
The masai people live on the high, dry grasslands of southern Kenya and northern Tanzania, where they raise cattle.

100

CENTRAL, EASTERN, AND SOUTHERN AFRICA

The southern half of the African continent includes hot and humid forests around the Equator, grasslands such as the East African savannah and the South African veldt, burning deserts, and high mountains. Volcanoes and lakes mark the course of the Great Rift Valley, a deep crack in the Earth's surface. Offshore, coral islands and reefs stretch eastwards into the Indian Ocean.

The Central African Republic lies at the heart of the continent, a small country with grassy highlands in the north and tropical forests in the southwest. The River Ubangi flows south into the River Congo, which divides the small country of Congo from its large southern neighbour, the Democratic Republic of the Congo (known as Zaïre from 1971 to 1997). The two Congolese capitals, Brazzaville and Kinshasa, lie on either side of the river. The country of Gabon stretches from the Congo border to the Atlantic Ocean. The Equator runs through these steamy lands of dense rain forest, which are home to many different peoples, including Pygmies. Many people travel by riverboat or canoe, especially when roads are washed away by the rains. In the east are the volcanic mountains of the Ruwenzori range. The Democratic Republic of the Congo has rich mineral resources including diamonds, but over the ages its wealth has been seized by colonial powers and corrupt rulers, leaving most people as poor farmers. The pop music of the region is listened to over a wide area of Africa.

On the Democratic Republic's eastern borders, the tiny countries of Rwanda and Burundi cling to steep slopes where bananas, corn, and beans are grown. These two countries have seen long years of conflict between the Hutu and Tutsi peoples who live there.

The course of Africa's Great Rift Valley is marked by deep lakes and volcanoes, stretching from Ethiopia to Malawi. Fossil remains of humans' earliest ancestors have been found in its rocky gorges. The region of East Africa stretches from the red, fertile farmland of Uganda, between Lake Albert and Lake Victoria, to the blue waters of the Indian Ocean. Somalia occupies the arid Horn of Africa, but to the south are the grassy plains of Kenya and Tanzania, dotted with acacia trees and patches of scrub. Beneath the snow-capped slopes of Mount Kilimanjaro, great herds of elephant, zebra, and wildebeeste still roam. East African farms produce sisal, vegetables, coffee, tea, and fruit,

▼ *The African elephant*
The world's biggest land mammal is found in many parts of Eastern and Southern Africa, where it is protected within national parks.

▶ *The smoke that thunders...*
That is one of the local names for the Victoria Falls, between Zimbabwe and Zambia. Three cascades are created where the bed of the River Zambezi drops by 400 feet.

◀ *Snap!*
The Nile crocodile is found through most of Africa. It grows into a ferocious adult, which can be well over 20 feet long. Crocodiles are also raised on special farms, for their hide.

and raise cattle. The island of Zanzibar is famous for its spices. Tourism is a growing industry. Hundreds of different African peoples live in East Africa, as well as some of European, Arab, and Indian descent. The Swahili language is understood over a large part of the region. Some East Africans live very traditional lives, while others work in modern cities such as Nairobi, Mombasa, or Dar-es-Salaam.

▼ Masai ornament
Beaded collars and earrings are the traditional dress of Masai women, who live across the Kenyan–Tanzanian border.

PARCHED EARTH

Between 30 and 90 miles across, the Namib desert follows the southwest African coast for over 700 miles. Rain hardly ever falls here, even though the air is often filled with fog where cold ocean currents meet the warm land mass.

South of Tanzania, beautiful tropical lands are crossed by the River Zambezi. The nations of Malawi, Mozambique, Zimbabwe, and Zambia include fertile farmlands growing tobacco, vegetables, and corn. There are also rich deposits of copper and other minerals. Botswana, in central Southern Africa, is largely given over to cattle ranching. It includes the Kalahari desert, home of the San people, and the great Okavango swamp. Southwestern nations include Angola and Namibia, where the harshness of the Namib desert resulted in its Atlantic region once being called the Skeleton Coast.

The Republic of South Africa is the continent's richest and most powerful country. It includes high grasslands and plateaus known as veld, the Drakensberg mountain range, and great cities such as Cape Town and Johannesburg. From 1950 to 1994 South Africa was divided by a racist policy called apartheid, which kept the Black majority from power. The mild climate of the south is ideal for growing grape vines and fruit. The country's wealth derives from its mineral resources, which include gold and diamonds. The population includes Zulus, Xhosa, Sotho, Afrikaners (the descendants of Dutch settlers), and Asians. South Africa's borders surround the small independent countries of Lesotho and Swaziland. Out in the Indian Ocean are the island nations of the Comoros, the Seychelles, Mauritius, and Africa's largest island, Madagascar.

▲ Sorghum crop, Zimbabwe
Hardy sorghum is a crop well adapted to the heat and occasional droughts of southeast African farms.

103

AUSTRALIA

▶ **Tracking the skies**
*Tidbinbilla Deep Space
Tracking Station, near
Canberra, is one of the three
most powerful receivers of
space signals in the world.*

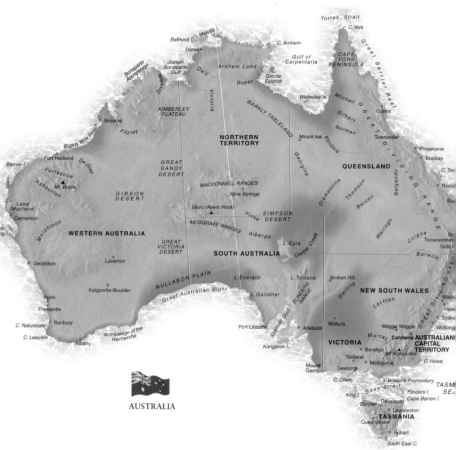

Torres Strait
C. York
Bathurst I.
Melville I.
Darwin
C. Arnhem
Gulf of
Carpentaria
CAPE
YORK
PENINSULA
Joseph
Bonaparte
Gulf
Arnhem Land
Daly
Groote
Eylandt
Roper
Bonaparte
Archipelago
Victoria
Wellesley Is.
Mitchell
GREAT BARRIER Reef
KIMBERLEY
PLATEAU
BARKLY TABLELAND
Gilbert
Cairns
Broome
Fitzroy
NORTHERN
TERRITORY
Mount Isa
Norman
Townsville
Eighty Mile Beach
Flinders
GREAT DIVIDING RANGE
Proserpine
Port Hedland
De Grey
GREAT
SANDY
DESERT
Mackay
Barrow I.
Fortescue
Mt. Bruce
QUEENSLAND
C. Tow
Ashburton
GIBSON
DESERT
MACDONNELL RANGES
Diamantina
Thomson
Belyando
Rockt
Lake
Macleod
Alice Springs
Barcoo
Bu
Carnarvon
Murchison
Uluru (Ayers Rock)
Finke
SIMPSON
DESERT
Warrego
irk I.
tog I.
WESTERN AUSTRALIA
MUSGRAVE RANGES
Alberga
L. Eyre
Culgoa
Toowoomba
GREAT
VICTORIA
DESERT
Coope Creek
SOUTH AUSTRALIA
Gold
Barwon
Geraldton
Laverton
L. Everard
L. Torrens
Broken Hill
NEW SOUTH WALES
NULLARBOR PLAIN
FLINDERS RANGE
Darling
Lachlan
Mala
Perth
Kalgoorlie-Boulder
Great Australian Bight
L. Gairdner
Sydi
Fremantle
Port Lincoln
Mildura
Wagga Wagga
Wollong
C. Naturaliste
Bunbury
Spencer Gulf
Adelaide
Murray
Canberra
AUSTRALIAN
CAPITAL
TERRITORY
C. Leeuwin
Albany
Archipelago of the
Recherche
Kangaroo I.
VICTORIA
Bendigo
Mt. Kosciusko
Ballarat
Melbourne
C. Howe
Mount
Gambier
Geelong
C. Otway
Wilson's Promontory
TASM
King I.
Bass Strait
Flinders I.
SE
Burnie
Davenport
Cape Barren I.
Launceston
TASMANIA
Queenstown
Hobart
South East C.

AUSTRALIA

▶ **City on the harbor**
*Sydney is Australia's biggest
city. Its beautiful harbor has
the world's widest long-span
bridge and an opera house
whose roofs look like billowing
sails.*

AUSTRALIA

This island is so huge that it is considered to be a landmass in its own right. Lying at the bottom of the world, between the Indian and Pacific Oceans, it is fringed to the east by the world's longest stretch of coral, the Great Barrier Reef. It includes several offshore islands, the biggest of which is Tasmania, across Bass Strait.

The interior of Australia is a wilderness like no other. Baked by intense heat, it is a very ancient land of glowing rocks and empty desert, of cracked earth and salt lakes. These are surrounded by a variety of landscapes, from rolling grasslands grazed by huge herds of sheep and cattle, to the tropical forests of the northeast where crocodiles lurk in muddy creeks, to southern scrubland and eucalyptus woods.

The Great Dividing Range runs parallel with the Pacific Coast, reaching 7,308 feet above sea level at Mount Kosciusko, in the Snowy Mountains. The Murray River rises here and flows 1,590 miles to Encounter Bay,

▲ *Cuddly koala*
The bear-like koala lives in eucalyptus or "gum trees." It has thick gray fur and weighs about 20 pounds.

joined on the way by its tributaries, the Lachlan, Murrumbidgee, Goulburn and Darling rivers.

The Australian coastline is indented by two huge bays, the Great Australian Bight, below the vast southern flatlands of the Nullarbor Plain, and in the north, the Gulf of Carpentaria, which divides Cape York Peninsula from Arnhem Land. The island of Tasmania includes mountains, temperate rain forests, and wild coastlines.

Australia has

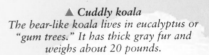

◀ *Sun and surf!*
Surfing is a passionate pastime for many Australians. Surfers Paradise, on Australia's eastern coast, is a favorite beach for riding the waves.

many animals and birds seen nowhere else on earth. They include the duck-billed platypus (an egg-laying river mammal), kangaroos and wallabies, who keep their babies in a pouch, wombats, deadly snakes and spiders, frilled lizards, and large flightless birds called emus.

Australia's cities turn their backs on the remote interior, which is known as the "Outback." Instead, they look outward to blue seas, where ocean breakers pound sandy beaches. The two biggest cities are Sydney and Melbourne, both in the southeast of the country. They are old rivals in business and trade. Brisbane is the chief city of the east, Adelaide of the south, and Perth of the west. The city of Canberra, surrounded by Australian Capital Territory (ACT), is a purpose-built capital centred on the federal parliament buildings.

Australia is divided into separate states, which have their own regional governments. Tropical Queensland grows sugarcane, pineapples, and bananas. New South Wales and Victoria produce the wool, meat, and dairy products that first brought prosperity to Australia. These two states include the chief centers of business, finance, and communications. Southern

▲ *Laughing Kookaburra*
This bird is the largest of the kingfishers. Its cackling call sounds just like laughter.

◀ *Flinders Street*
This fine old train station, just to the north of the Yarra River, links central Melbourne with its sprawling suburbs.

Australia grows grapes and produces excellent wines. Tasmania has a timber industry, often challenged by conservation campaigners. It also raises livestock and grows apples and pears. Minerals are important in Western Australia and the remote Northern Territory. Tourism is a growing industry throughout Australia. Popular sports include Australian Rules football, rugby football, cricket, and tennis.

Descendants of the first Australians are called Aborigines. Their ancestors entered the land across the Torres Strait from perhaps 50,000 years ago. They became experts at surviving in harsh environments and were skilled hunters with spear and boomerang. Some groups were nomadic while others were settled. A rich body of myths and legends grew up among the Aborigines, who still look back to a magical "Dreamtime."

In the 1600s Dutch navigators began to explore the Australian coast. In 1770 the English sea captain James Cook claimed New South Wales for Great Britain. The first colonists were prisoners sent out from Britain, but soon many other British people arrived to farm or search for gold. The Aborigines were persecuted and murdered and their lands were stolen. They have faced a long struggle to regain their lands and to achieve civil rights.

Today's Australians include people of many different backgrounds and cultures. There

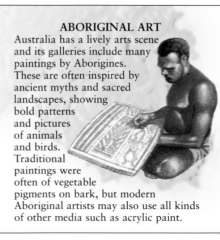

ABORIGINAL ART
Australia has a lively arts scene and its galleries include many paintings by Aborigines. These are often inspired by ancient myths and sacred landscapes, showing bold patterns and pictures of animals and birds. Traditional paintings were often of vegetable pigments on bark, but modern Aboriginal artists may also use all kinds of other media such as acrylic paint.

are Irish, Italians, Greeks, Dutch, Scandinavians, Lebanese, Vietnamese, Thais, and Indians in addition to the Australians of Aboriginal and British descent. Australia has retained close cultural links with Great Britain, but is considering breaking its historical ties with the British monarchy to become a republic. It increasingly sees itself as a major economic power of the Pacific Rim.

▲ *In the Victorian Alps*
The Horn of Mount Buffalo towers over a plateau in northeastern Victoria. The region is popular with skiers and walkers.

North Cape

Whangerei

Gt. Barrier Island

Auckland

Manukau

Bay of
Plenty

East Cape

Waikato

Hamilton

Rotorua

NORTH
ISLAND

L. Taupo

Gisborne

New Plymouth

Ruapehu

Napier

Wanganui

Hastings

Palmerston North

Cape Farewell

Nelson

Cook Strait

Wellington

Westport

Blenheim

Greymouth

SOUTHERN ALPS

SOUTH
ISLAND

Mt. Cook

Canterbury
Plains

Christchurch

Timaru

Clutha

Dunedin

Foveaux Strait

Invercargill

Stewart Island

NEW ZEALAND

▶ *Tropical cascade*
A waterfall drops through the lush New Guinea
forest. Giant butterflies and birds of paradise
flourish in the island's humid climate.

▶ *Welcome to Bora Bora*
This is one of the Society Islands in
French Polynesia. The region includes
many volcanic peaks and forested valleys.

NEW ZEALAND AND THE PACIFIC

The Pacific Ocean is the largest in the world, covering about one third of the world's surface. It gives its name to Oceania, the group of lands which includes Australia, Papua New Guinea, New Zealand and the thousands of tiny islands scattered across the ocean. Another name for this region is Australasia.

▲ *Canoes of the Pacific*
Trobriand Islanders crew a trading canoe.
Canoes are the traditional method of
travel between Pacific islands.

Papua New Guinea (PNG) occupies the eastern half of the island of New Guinea and also includes many smaller islands, such as New Britain, New Ireland, and the northern Solomons. The country includes forested hills and remote valleys, the home of hundreds of different peoples speaking many languages. The highest point in all Oceania is Mount Wilhelm, 14,789 feet above sea level. PNG is rich in copper and exports coffee, tea and rubber.

New Zealand lies about 1,200 miles to the southeast of Australia. It is a group of islands, of which the two largest, North and South, are divided by Cook Strait. The islands were settled over a thousand years ago by a Polynesian people called the Maoris. The islands were also discovered by the English explorer James Cook in 1769, and by the 1800s the islands were being colonized by British whalers, farmers, prospectors, and traders.

The capital, Wellington, and the largest city, Auckland, are both on North Island. Like many other islands around the Pacific, this is volcanic and has

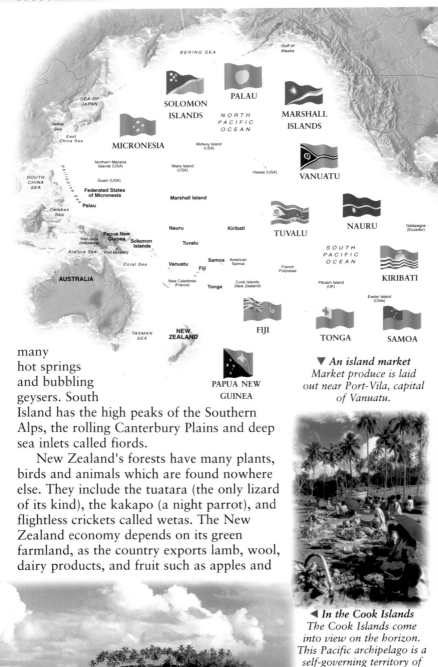

BERING SEA

Gulf of Alaska

SEA OF JAPAN

SOLOMON ISLANDS

PALAU

NORTH PACIFIC OCEAN

MARSHALL ISLANDS

Yellow Sea

East China Sea

MICRONESIA

Midway Island (USA)

VANUATU

SOUTH CHINA SEA

Northern Mariana Islands (USA)

Wake Island (USA)

Hawaii (USA)

Guam (USA)

Federated States of Micronesia

Marshall Island

Galapagos (Ecuador)

NAURU

Celebes Sea

Palau

Nauru

Kiribati

TUVALU

Iran Jaya (Indonesia)

Papua New Guinea

Solomon Islands

Tuvalu

SOUTH PACIFIC OCEAN

Arafura Sea

Port Moresby

Coral Sea

Vanuatu

Samoa

American Samoa

KIRIBATI

AUSTRALIA

Fiji

French Polynesia

New Caledonia (France)

Tonga

Cook Islands (New Zealand)

Pitcairn Island (UK)

Easter Island (Chile)

TASMAN SEA

NEW ZEALAND

FIJI

TONGA

SAMOA

PAPUA NEW GUINEA

many hot springs and bubbling geysers. South Island has the high peaks of the Southern Alps, the rolling Canterbury Plains and deep sea inlets called fiords.

New Zealand's forests have many plants, birds and animals which are found nowhere else. They include the tuatara (the only lizard of its kind), the kakapo (a night parrot), and flightless crickets called wetas. The New Zealand economy depends on its green farmland, as the country exports lamb, wool, dairy products, and fruit such as apples and

▼ *An island market*
Market produce is laid out near Port-Vila, capital of Vanuatu.

◄ *In the Cook Islands*
The Cook Islands come into view on the horizon. This Pacific archipelago is a self-governing territory of New Zealand.

▲ Putting on a show
Traditionally, many peoples on New Guinea wear body paint, feathers, bones, grass, and leaves for special dances and festivals.

reserves—the island of Nauru has been mined for phosphates on a devastating scale. Cruise liners bring tourists to islands such as Tahiti in French Polynesia.

The peoples of the Pacific fall into three main groups. The Melanesians are the peoples of the west, such as the Solomon Islanders. The Micronesians come from the Marshall and Caroline Islands. The Polynesians have spread right across the ocean from Hawaii to New Zealand. Some islands have also been settled by people of European and Asian descent.

pears. Factories produce textiles and plastics and most New Zealanders enjoy a high standard of living.

Many chains of islands dot the vast expanse of the South Pacific. Some are ruled by other nations, but others have joined together to form their own countries. Independent Pacific nations include the Federated States of Micronesia, Palau, the Marshall Islands, Kiribati (pronounced Kiribass), Nauru, the Solomon Islands, Tuvalu, Fiji, Tonga, Vanuatu, and Western Samoa.

Most islands of the Pacific are formed from coral or from volcanic rock. Many have villages bordering peaceful blue lagoons and offshore reefs. Coconut palms provide food (often dried and exported as copra), fiber for matting and leaves for roofing. Crops include bananas, vanilla pods, sweet potatoes and taro. Many islanders raise pigs and chickens and catch fish such as tuna. Some islands have mineral

KIWIFRUIT
More kiwifruit are grown in New Zealand than anywhere else in the world. They are round and soft, with slightly furry skins. Inside they are sweet, green, and fleshy. They have become very popular for use in desserts, cakes, and salads. Exports of kiwifruit now bring New Zealand more money than cheese or apples. The success is due to clever marketing. Growers named the fruit after the flightless bird which is the national emblem. "Kiwi" is also a nickname for any New Zealander.

▲ **Across the ice**
*Adélie penguins return to the
same breeding grounds each
year, shuffling and sliding
over the Antarctic ice.*

S. Orkney Is

C. Norvegia

S. Shetland Is

Maud Land

Enderby Land

Antarctic
Peninsula

WEDELL
SEA

Coats Land

Palmer
Archipelago

Mac Robertson Land   Cape
Darnley

Alexander I.

Palmer Land

Berkner I.
Ronne
Ice Shelf

PR. CHARLES MTNS.

Charcot I.

PENSACOLA
MTNS.

AMERICAN
HIGHLAND

BELLINGHAUSEN
SEA

Vinson
Massif

South Pole

GREATER
ANTARCTICA

Queen
Mary
Land

Ellsworth
Land

LESSER
ANTARCTICA

TRANSANTARCTIC MTNS.

Knox Coast

Thurston I.

Wilkes Land

AMUNDSEN
SEA

Mt. Kirkpatrick ▲

Siple I.

Marie Byrd
Land

Ross Ice
Shelf

Roosevelt I. ▲

Victoria Land

Mt. Erebus ▲

George V
Land

ROSS
SEA

C. Adare

South ★
Magnetic
Pole

▲ **Southern elephant seal**
*This blubbery giant can weigh as much
as a truck. It breeds on the bleak islands
of the southern oceans, such as South
Georgia, Kerguelen, and Macquarie.*

ANTARCTICA

The southernmost point on Earth, the South Pole, lies at the center of a frozen landmass called Antarctica. This is the coldest and windiest place on Earth, ringed by great sheets of ice.

Nobody has ever settled in Antarctica permanently, but explorers have mapped its icy wilderness and scientists visit special bases to study the climate and geology. Even a few tourists have started to come here, attracted by spectacular sights such as Mount Erebus, an active volcano. The Vinson Massif reaches 16,062 feet above sea level, while the rock of the Bentley Trench is 8,325 feet below sea level – the lowest point on the Earth's crust.

The whole land is buried in deep ice, nearly 3 miles thick in places. The seas around the coasts are frozen too, forming great shelves of ice. Massive slabs break off to form icebergs in the southern spring (when the northern part of the Earth is experiencing autumn).

▲ *Ready to dive!*
A humpback whale often slaps the water with its giant tail flukes, making a noise that can be heard several miles away.

Antarctica is not part of any country, although several nations claim sections of the territory. Many people believe it should remain under international control and that the rich minerals thought to lie beneath its surface should be left alone. No plants or animals live in the interior, but the southern oceans are rich in sea life, and colonies of penguins and schools of whales may be seen around the coast and islands.

◀ *Weather watch*
A balloon is released from an Antarctic weather station. Antarctica is a good place for scientists to study the state of the ozone layer.

POLAR LANDS

▶ **Modern homes**
*With little timber to
be had for building,
traditional Inuit
homes were made of
turf and stone. Today,
ready-made housing
may be imported and
raised on site.*

Yukon

Bering Strait

**ALASKA
(USA)**

*CHUKCHI
SEA*

Ambarchik

Kolyma

Mackenzie

Barrow · Pt. Barrow

*EAST
SIBERIAN
SEA*

Indigirka

**R
U
S
S
I
A**

*BEAUFORT
SEA*

C.Bathurst

New
Siberian
Islands

Lena

**C
A
N
A
D
A**

Banks
Island

McClure Strait

*ARCTIC
OCEAN*

*LAPTEV
SEA*

Victoria
Island

Nordvik

Queen
Elizabeth
Islands

★North Magnetic Pole

Severnaya
Zemlya

★North Pole

Yenisey

Ellesmere
Island

Dikson

Foxe
Basin

*LINCOLN
SEA*

Franz
Josef
Land

Baffin Island

Baffin
Bay

Novaja Zemlya

*KARA
SEA*

Ob'

Davis Strait

**GREENLAND
(DENMARK)**

Svalbard
(Norway)

*BARENTS
SEA*

Pechora

Godthåb

*GREENLAND
SEA*

North Cape

Murmansk

Denmark Strait

ICELAND

*NORWEGIAN
SEA*

Archangel

Reykjavik

▶ **Frostbite warning**
*The cold of the Arctic is severe and can
be extremely dangerous. In central
Greenland, temperatures can drop to an
incredible -70°F.*

THE ARCTIC

The northernmost point on our planet is called the North Pole. It lies at the centre of the Arctic Ocean, which is permanently covered in a thick ice cap. Bordering the ocean are the bitterly cold coasts of North America, Europe and Asia.

To reach the North Pole, you either have to travel beneath it in a submarine or cross over the ice cap, battling through fierce blizzards. The countries around this frozen sea take in the U.S. state of Alaska, the maze of islands which make up the Canadian Arctic, Greenland, Norway, Sweden, Finland, and the long coastline of the Russian Federation.

These lands include high mountains and frozen snowy plains known as tundra. The topsoil of the tundra melts in the brief northern summer, and wildflowers blossom amongst the pools of water. At midsummer the Arctic stays light for 24 hours of the day, and at midwinter the

▲ *The caribou*
This reindeer migrates across forests and tundra in vast herds. It is still hunted by the peoples of the American Arctic.

night is endless. Whales, seals, walruses, and polar bears swim in the rich Arctic seas.

Many peoples have settled in the Arctic, traditionally living by hunting and fishing or by herding reindeer. Today some of them work in oil production or fish processing factories. Arctic peoples include the Aleuts of Alaska, the Inuit communities of northern Canada and Greenland (Kalaallit), the Saami of northern Scandinavia, the Evenks, Chukchi, Yukagirs, Khants, Nenets, and many other groups of the Russian Federation.

▼ *Dried fish*
Fish are preserved by natural drying in many communities. Cod, Arctic char and capelin are all caught in polar waters.

Country	Area sq miles	Population millions	Capital	Economy 1999
EUROPE: The Far North p.13				
Denmark	26,766	5.3	Copenhagen	bacon, butter
Finland	209,426	5.1	Helsinki	timber, paper
Iceland	64,002	0.3	Reykjavik	fish
Norway	201,264	4.4	Oslo	oil, timber, fish
Sweden	279,494	8.9	Stockholm	steel, paper
Other territories: Faeroe Islands, Jan Mayen, Svalbard				
EUROPE: Low Countries p.17				
Belgium	18,964	10.2	Brussels	steel, textiles
Luxembourg	1,606	0.4	Luxembourg	steel, banking
Netherlands	25,576	15.6	Amsterdam	dairy, bulbs
EUROPE: The British Isles p.21				
Republic of Ireland	42,810	3.6	Dublin	dairy, beer
United Kingdom of Great Britain & Northern Ireland				
England	81,000	49	London	foods, cars
Scotland	48,934	5	Edinburgh	oil, whisky
Wales	12,900	3	Cardiff	lamb, tourism
N Ireland	8,792	2	Belfast	machinery
Total	151,626	59		finance
Other territories: Isle of Man, Guernsey, Jersey				
EUROPE: France and Monaco p.25				
France	338,018	58.6	Paris	wine, fashion
Monaco	1.2	028	Monaco	chemicals
EUROPE: Germany and the Alps p.29				
Austria	852,106	8.1	Vienna	timber, tourism
Germany	221,736	82	Berlin	cars, finance
Liechtenstein	99	0.03	Vaduz	tourism
Switzerland	25,654	7.1	Bern	cheese, banking
EUROPE: The Iberian Peninsula p.33				
Andorra	288	0.06	Andorra la Viella	tourism
Portugal	56,937	9.9	Lisbon	wine, tourism
Spain	313,726	39.3	Madrid	wine, tourism
Other territories: Gibraltar				
EUROPE: Italy and its Neighbors p.37				
Italy	187,190	57.4	Rome	wine, cars
Malta	196	0.4	Valletta	dockyards

Country	Area sq miles	Population millions,	Capital	Economy 1999
San Marino	37	0.02	San Marino	tourism
Vatican City	0.27	0.001	Vatican City	Catholic Church

EUROPE: Central Europe p.41

Country	Area sq miles	Population millions,	Capital	Economy 1999
Czech Republic	49,000	10.3	Prague	beer, glass
Estonia	28,024	1.5	Tallinn	oil, timber, pork
Hungary	57,807	10.2	Budapest	fruit, wine
Latvia	39,582	2.5	Riga	machines, dairy
Lithuania	40,514	3.7	Vilnius	machines, pork
Poland	194,298	38.6	Warsaw	coal, copper
Slovakia	30,469	5.4	Bratislava	mining, foods

EUROPE: The Balkans p.45

Country	Area sq miles	Population millions,	Capital	Economy 1999
Albania	17,864	3.4	Tiranë	fruit, mining
Bosnia- Herzegovina	31,770	3.6	Sarajevo	garments, chemicals
Bulgaria	68,911	8.3	Sofia	tobacco, textiles
Croatia	35,133	4.8	Zagreb	machines, chemicals
Greece	82,013	10.5	Athens	tourism, shipping
Macedonia (Former Yugoslav Republic)	15,978	2.1	Skopje	food, textiles
Romania	23,302	22.5	Bucharest	petrochemicals
Slovenia	12,883	2	Ljubljana	timber, vegetables
Yugoslavia (Serbia-Montenegro)	63,487	10.6	Belgrade	textiles, steel

EUROPE/ASIA: Russia and its Neighbors p.49

Country	Area sq miles	Population millions,	Capital	Economy 1999
Armenia	18,641	3.8	Yerevan	fruit, nuts, mining
Azerbaijan	54,060	7.6	Baku	oil, natural gas
Belarus	129,248	10.3	Minsk	petrochemicals
Georgia	43,310	5.4	Tbilisi	food, machines
Kazakhstan	1,688,498	16.4	Almaty	oil, wool
Kyrgyzstan	123,345	4.6	Bishkek	wool, cotton
Moldova	20,940	4.3	Chisinau	food, tobacco
Russian Federation	10,612,070	147.3	Moscow	wheat, iron ore
Tajikistan	88,920	6	Dushanbe	cotton, textiles
Turkmenistan	303,295	4.6	Askhabad	oil, cotton
Ukraine	375,132	50.7	Kiev	wheat, machines
Uzbekistan	278,009	23.7	Tashkent	cotton

NORTH AND CENTRAL AMERICA: Greenland and Canada p.53

Country	Area sq miles	Population millions,	Capital	Economy 1999
Canada	6,165,652	30.1	Ottawa	timber, wheat

Other territories: Greenland, St. Pierre & Miquelon

Country	Area sq miles	Population millions	Capital	Economy 1999

NORTH AND CENTRAL AMERICA: United States of America p.57

USA	5,818,138	267.7	Washington, DC	wheat, coal, oil

NORTH AND CENTRAL AMERICA: Mexico, Central America, & Caribbean p.63

Country	Area sq miles	Population millions	Capital	Economy
Mexico	1,225,716	95.7	Mexico City	oil, vehicles
Central Belize	14,270	0.2	Belmopan	timber, fruit
Costa Rica	31,628	3.5	San José	coffee, bananas
El Salvador	13,294	5.9	San Salvador	coffee, corn
Guatemala	67,662	11.2	Guatemala City	coffee, bananas
Honduras	69,648	5.8	Tegucigalpa	coffee, bananas
Nicaragua	91,965	4.4	Managua	coffee, cotton
Panama	48,788	2.7	Panama City	bananas, sugar

Caribbean & North Atlantic

Country	Area sq miles	Population millions	Capital	Economy
Antigua & Barbuda	274	0.1	Saint John's	sugar, cotton
Bahamas	8,646	0.3	Freeport	banking, tourism
Barbados	267	0.3	Bridgetown	sugar
Cuba	71,164	11.1	Havana	sugar, coffee
Dominica	466	0.1	Roseau	bananas
Dominican Republic	30,100	8.2	Santo Domingo	sugar, coffee
Grenada	214	0.1	St. George's	spices
Haiti	17,243	6.6	Port-au-Prince	sugar, coffee
Jamaica	885	2.6	Kingston	sugar, tourism
St. Kitts-Nevis	155	0.04	Basseterre	sugar, cotton
St. Lucia	382	0.1	St. Lucia	tourism, bananas
St. Vincent & the Grenadines	241	0.1	Kingstown	bananas, copra
Trinidad & Tobago	3,187	1.3	Port-of -Spain	petrochemicals

Other territories: Anguilla, Aruba, Bermuda, British Virgin Islands, Cayman Islands, Guadeloupe, Martinique, Montserrat, Netherlands Antilles, Puerto Rico, Turks & Caicos Islands, US Virgin Islands

SOUTH AMERICA: The Northern Andes p.67

Country	Area sq miles	Population millions	Capital	Economy
Bolivia	682,644	7.8	La Paz/Sucre	coffee, tin
Colombia	707,708	37.4	Bogotá	coffee, emeralds
Ecuador	286,755	12	Quito	coffee, fishmeal
Peru	798,617	24.4	Lima	lead, fishmeal

SOUTH AMERICA: Brazil and its Neighbors p.71

Country	Area sq miles	Population millions	Capital	Economy
Brazil	5,289,234	160.3	Brasília	coffee, iron ore
Guyana	133,579	0.8	Georgetown	sugar, bauxite
Suriname	101,795	0.4	Paramaribo	sugar, bauxite

Country	Area sq miles	Population millions,	Capital	Economy 1999
Venezuela	566,733	22.6	Caracas	oil, coffee

Other territories: French Guiana

SOUTH AMERICA: Argentina and its Neighbors p.75

Argentina	1,727,515	35.6	Buenos Aires	beef, hides
Chile	457,900	14.6	Santiago	wine, fruit
Paraguay	252,749	5.1	Asunción	beef, cotton
Uruguay	47,355	3.2	Montevideo	beef, hides

Other territories: Falkland Islands (Malvinas), South Georgia & South Sandwich Islands

ASIA: Southwest p.79

Bahrain	410	0.6	Manamah	oil
Cyprus	5,747	0.7	Nicosia	tourism, fruit
Iran	1,024,047	67.5	Teheran	oil, carpets
Iraq	272,444	21.2	Baghdad	oil, dates
Israel	12,906	5.8	Jerusalem	fruit, vegetables
Jordan	59,653	4.4	Amman	phosphates
Kuwait	15,087	1.8	Kuwait City	oil
Lebanon	6,462	3.9	Beirut	textiles, fruit
Oman	168,986	2.3	Muscat	oil, fishing
Qatar	7,105	0.6	Doha	oil, fertilizers
Saudi Arabia	1,491,890	19.5	Riyadh	oil, dates
Syria	115,379	15	Damascus	oil, cotton
Turkey (partly in Europe)	484,340	63.7	Ankara	tobacco, textiles
United Arab Emirates (UAE)	46,696	2.3	Abu Dhabi	oil, natural gas
Yemen	328,074	15.2	San'a	oil, fishing

ASIA: India and its Neighbors p.83

Afghanistan	405,284	22.1	Kabul	carpets, gas
Bangladesh	89,479	122.2	Dhaka	jute, tea
Bhutan	28,969	0.8	Thimphu	timber, rice
India	1,967,830	969.7	Delhi	cotton, tea
Maldives	185	0.3	Malé	fishing
Nepal	87,873	22.6	Kathmandu	tourism, timber
Pakistan	499,558	137.8	Islamabad	cotton, rice
Sri Lanka	40,769	18.7	Colombo	tea, rubber

Other territories: British Indian Ocean territory

Country	Area sq miles	Population millions	Capital	Economy 1999
ASIA: China and its Neighbors p.87				
China	5,963,462	1,236.7	Beijing	rice, tea, manufacture
Korea (North)	76,000	24.3	Pyongyang	coal, textiles
Korea (South)	61,172	45.9	Seoul	vehicles, manufacture
Mongolia	351,084	2.4	Ulan Bator	wool
Taiwan	22,363	21.5	Taipei	electronics, plastics
Other territories: Macao (reverts to China 1999), Paracel Islands, Spratly Islands				
ASIA: Japan p.91				
Japan	229,727	126.1	Tokyo	cars, electronics
ASIA: Southeast Asia p.93				
Brunei	3,582	0.3	Bandar Seri Begawan	oil, natural gas
Cambodia	112,741	11.2	Phnom Penh	rubber, timber
Indonesia	1,192,720	204.3	Jakarta	oil, rubber
Laos	147,098	5.1	Vientiane	timber, coffee
Malaysia	206,900	21	Kuala Lumpur	timber, rubber
Myanmar (Burma)	421,319	46.8	Yangon	timber, rice, rubber
Philippines	186,416	73.4	Manila	garments, electronics
Singapore	382	3.5	Singapore City	finance, shipping
Thailand	319,393	60.1	Bangkok	tourism, rice
Vietnam	204,787	75.1	Hanoi	rice, coal
AFRICA: North and West Africa p.97				
North Africa				
Algeria	1,479,988	29.8	Algiers	oil, olives
Egypt	621,543	64.8	Cairo	cotton, tourism
Eritrea	56,919	3.6	Asmara	hides, gum arabic
Libya	1,093,357	5.6	Tripoli	oil
Morocco	286,009	28.2	Rabat	phosphates, dates
Tunisia	102,000	9.3	Tunis	oil, fruits, tourism
Western Sahara	156,664	0.2	El Aaiún	phosphates
Sub-Sahara				
Burkina Faso	170,336	10.9	Ouagadougou	cotton, cattle
Chad	798,862	7	N'Djamena	cotton, cattle
Djibouti	14,416	0.6	Djibouti	hides, port facilities
Ethiopia	686,198	58.7	Addis Ababa	coffee, hides
Mali	770,608	9.9	Bamako	cotton, peanuts
Mauritania	640,464	2.4	Nouakchott	gypsum, fish
Niger	737,221	9.8	Niamey	cattle, vegetables
Sudan	1,557,083	27.9	Khartoum	cotton, gum arabic

Country	Area sq miles	Population millions	Capital	Economy 1999
West Africa				
Benin	69,980	5.9	Porto-Novo	cotton, peanuts
Cameroon	295,470	13.9	Yaoundé	cotton, peanuts
Cape Verde Islands	2,700	0.4	Praia	fish, bananas
Côte d'Ivoire	200,375	15	Abidjan	cocoa, coffee
Equatorial Guinea	17,429	0.4	Malabo	cocoa, coffee, timber
Gambia	6,642	1.2	Banjul	fish, peanuts
Ghana	148,079	18.1	Accra	gold, cocoa
Guinea	152,771	7.5	Conakry	bauxite, coffee
Guinea-Bissau	22,447	0.1	Bissau	fish, peanuts
Liberia	69,204	2.3	Monrovia	diamonds, palm-oil
Nigeria	574,069	107.1	Abuja	oil, cotton, peanuts
Senegal	122,239	8.8	Dakar	fish, peanuts
Sierra Leone	44,941	4.4	Freetown	diamonds, cocoa
Togo	35,285	4.7	Lomé	phosphates, cotton

AFRICA: Central, Eastern, and Southern Africa p.101

Country	Area sq miles	Population millions	Capital	Economy 1999
Central Africa				
Burundi	17,296	6.1	Bujumbura	coffee, tea
Central African Republic	388,352	.3	Bangui	cotton, timber
Congo	212,514	2.6	Brazzaville	cocoa, timber
Congo (Democratic Republic, formerly Zaïre)	1,457,410	47.4	Kinshasa	diamonds, copper
Gabon	166,323	1.2	Libreville	oil, timber
Rwanda	16,361	7.7	Kigali	coffee, tea
São Tomé and Príncipe	599	0.1	São Tomé	cocoa, bananas
Eastern Africa				
Comoros	1,155	0.6	Moroni	copra, spices, fish
Kenya	388,352	28.8	Nairobi	tourism, coffee
Seychelles	251	0.1	Victoria	tourism, copra, fish
Somalia	396,234	10.2	Mogadishu	livestock, bananas
Tanzania	583,955	29.5	Dodoma	tourism, sisal, cloves
Uganda	147,000	20.6	Kampala	coffee, cotton
Southern Africa				
Angola	774,684	11.6	Luanda	coffee, diamonds
Botswana	357,298	1.5	Gaborone	cattle, hides
Lesotho	18,856	2	Maseru	wool, cattle
Madagascar	369,216	14.1	Antananarivo	coffee, spices, sugar
Malawi	58,460	9.6	Lilongwe	tobacco, cotton
Mauritius	1,158	1.1	Port Louis	sugar, tea, garments

Country	Area sq miles	Population millions	Capital	Economy 1997
Mozambique	487,637	18.4	Maputo	cashew nuts, cotton
Namibia	512,207	1.7	Windhoek	uranium, diamonds
South Africa	758,618	42.5	Cape Town, Pretoria	gold, diamonds
Swaziland	10,790	1	Mbabane	fruit, sugar
Zambia	467,666	9.4	Lusaka	copper, lead, tobacco
Zimbabwe	242,537	11.4	Harare	tobacco, vegetables

Atlantic Ocean territories: St Helena & dependencies

Indian Ocean territories: Mayotte, Réunion

OCEANIA: Australia p.105

Australia	4,773,690	18.5	Canberra	wool, minerals, tourism

Other territories: Ashmore & Cartier Islands, Christmas Island, Cocos (Keeling) Islands, Coral sea Islands, Heard & Macdonald Islands, Norfolk Island

OCEANIA: New Zealand and the Pacific p.109

Federated States of				
Micronesia	436	0.1	Kolonia	copra, fishing
Fiji	11,390	0.8	Suva	sugar, fishing
Kiribati	425	0.025	Bairiki	copra, fishing
Marshall Islands	112	0.1	Majuro	copra, phosphates
Nauru	13	0.01	Yaren	phosphates
New Zealand	164,761	3.6	Wellington	meat, wool, fruit
Palau	304	0.02	Koror	copra, fishing
Papua New Guinea	287,603	4.4	Port Moresby	coffee, cocoa, copper
Solomon Islands	18,311	0.4	Honiara	copra, fishing
Tonga	434	0.1	Nukualofa	copra, vanilla
Tuvalu	14	0.013	Funafuti	copra, fishing
Vanuatu	9,174	0.2	Porta-Vila	copra, livestock
Western Samoa	1,764	0.2	Apia	copra, fishing

Pacific territories: American Samoa, Baker & Howard islands, Cook Islands, French Polynesia, Guam, Jarvis Island, Johnston Atoll, Kingman Reef, Midway Islands, New Caledonia, Niue, Northern Marianas, Pitcairn, Tokelau, Wake Island, Wallis & Futuna

Southern ocean territories: Bouvet Island, French Southern & Antarctic Territories

INDEX

123

Acknowledgments

The publishers would like to thank the following artists who contributed to this book:

Julie Banyard, Janos Marffy, Josephine Martin, Terry Riley, Guy Smith and Michael White.

Our thanks to Keith Lye for the use of his photographs on pages 68 (B/L); 79 (B/L); 80 (C); 81 (B); 84 (T/R); 88 (T/L); 97 (T/L); 98 (T/L)

Other photographs are from MKP Archives.